Mastering Academic Reading

LAWRENCE J. ZWIER

Michigan State University

Contributions by
MATTHEW S. WELTIG

Ann Arbor
The University of Michigan Press

Copyright © by the University of Michigan 2010
All rights reserved
Published in the United States of America
The University of Michigan Press
Manufactured in the United States of America

∞ Printed on acid-free paper

ISBN-13: 978-0-472-03223-5

2013   2012   2011   2010   4   3   2   1

Acknowledgments

The author would like to thank:

William Grabe and Fredricka Stoller, for their perceptive and practical work on L2 reading. From the very inception of the idea for this book, I knew it would owe a lot to them.

Kelly Sippell, for the whole idea of a challenging, truly advanced reading text. I cannot list all of the ways in which she sustained this book. She has my deepest respect and gratitude.

Matthew Weltig, an excellent writer and great colleague, for his indispensable contributions to this book.

Robyn Brinks Lockwood for her help in developing the manuscript to its fullest potential.

Grateful acknowledgment is given to the following authors, publishers, and journals for permission to reprint previously published materials.

American Scientist Magazine for "Early Canid Domestication: The Farm Fox Experiment," by Lyudmila N. Trut, *American Scientist* 87, March–April 1999, 160–169. Copyright © 1999.

Elsevier for "Extremes of human heat tolerance: life at the precipice of thermoregulatory failure," by W. Larry Kenney, David W. DeGroot, and Lacy Alexander Holowatz, from *Journal of Thermal Biology*, Vol. 29, Issues 7-8, October–December, 2004. Copyright © 2004.

Massachusetts Institute of Technology and American Institute of Aeronautics and Astronautics for "Scalability and Evolutionary Dynamics of Air Transportation Networks in the United States," by Philippe A. Bonnefoy and R. John Hansman, Jr. for the 7th AIAA Aviation Technology, Integration and Operations Conference, September 2007. Copyright © 2007.

Minnesota Department of Natural Resources for *Hypothermia . . . The Cold Facts*, by Timothy M. Smalley, 2007. Copyright © 2007.

Nature Publishing Group for the book review of *The Biology of Human Survival: Life and Death in Extreme Environments* by Mike Stroud, *Nature* 431, 2004. Copyright © 2004.

Penguin for the adapted excerpts from *Collapse: How Societies Choose to Fail or Succeed* by Jared Diamond, 2005. Copyright © 2005 by Jared Diamond. Used by permission of Viking Penguin, a division of the Penguin Group (USA), Inc.

Random House for the excerpt from *The Botany of Desire: A Plant's Eye View* by Michael Pollan; copyright © 2001 by Michael Pollan. Used by permission of Random House, Inc.

Random House for the excerpt from *The Island of Lost Maps: A True Story of Cartographic Crime* by Miles Harvey, 2000. Copyright © 2000 by Miles Harvey. Used by permission of Random House, Inc.

United Nations Food and Agriculture Organization for the data for the table "Worst Deforestation Rate of Primary Forests, 2000–2005, All Countries" at www.mongabay.com, 2006. Copyright © Rhett A. Butler 2008.

The U.S. Centennial of Flight Commission for "Deregulation and Its Consequences" by Asif Siddiqi at www.cintennialofflight.gov.

University of Michigan Press for the adapted excerpt from *Category 5: The Story of Camille: Lessons Unlearned from America's Most Violent Hurricane* by Ernest Zebrowski and Judith A. Howard, 2005. Copyright © 2005, University of Michigan.

Contents

To the Teacher and Student

Mastering Academic Reading (MAR) is meant to challenge advanced-level students of English for Academic Purposes (EAP). The units and the readings within them are long. The comprehension and expansion exercises are demanding. The desired outcome is that MAR-trained EAP students will be able to better hold their own in university classes where the reading volume and vocabulary demands are high.

The conception of this book owes a lot to William Grabe and Fredricka Stoller and their superb analysis of L1 and L2 reading practices in *Teaching and Researching Reading* (2002). It would be hard to articulate all of the ways in which Grabe and Stoller got EAP reading right, but a few core principles are detailed.

Rapid and automatic access to vocabulary is absolutely prime. As Grabe and Stoller put it,

> For good readers, lexical access is automatic. In addition to being very fast, it cannot be readily reflected on consciously, and it cannot be suppressed (a good definition of **automaticity**); that is, when the eye sees a word, the reader cannot stop him or herself from accessing its meaning. Both rapid processing and automaticity in word recognition (for a large number of words) typically require thousands of hours of practice in reading. (p. 21)

Though L1 research underlies this observation, they intend it to inform instruction in L2 reading as well.

The three main purposes for academic reading are as follows.

- **Reading to learn** (reading in order to perform some other task, such as writing a report)
- **Reading to integrate information, write, and critique texts**
- **Reading for basic comprehension**

In most real-life academic situations, the boundaries among these purposes blur. It's difficult to say, for example, where basic comprehension stops and the "critiquing" purpose comes to the fore. Grabe and Stoller call attention to the great importance of mental "models" in integrating, writing, and critiquing, especially "longer text" and "field" models. Both of these reflect an understanding of how knowledge acquired from a reading fits into patterns—not just a pattern of information within the text but also a pattern of relationships with other texts and "the real world."

Grabe and Stoller point out that reading for basic comprehension, though definitionally "basic," is not crude or intellectually simple:

> Reading for general comprehension, when accomplished by a skilled fluent reader, requires very rapid and automatic processing of words, strong skills in forming a general meaning representation of main ideas, and efficient coordination of many processes under very limited time constraints.
>
> These abilities are often taken for granted by fluent readers because they usually occur automatically; that is, we make use of these abilities without giving them much thought if we are fluent readers. In L2 contexts, however, the difficulties that students have in becoming fluent readers of longer texts under time constraints reveal the complexities of reading for general comprehension. Because of its demands for processing efficiency, reading for general understanding may at times even be more difficult to master than reading to learn, an ability that is often assumed to be a more difficult extension of general comprehension abilities. (This misperception is most likely due to the ways in which reading comprehension and reading to learn are commonly tested in schools.) (p. 14–15)

You have probably noticed the emphasis Grabe and Stoller place on **the need to read—and read a lot.** This poses an enormous problem for EAP programs and for EAP materials writers. How do you provide, assign, check comprehension of, and base tasks on enough material? In short, how do you get students to read enough? We have no illusion that we have solved the problem with MAR, but we have at least faced it. We provide a lot of reading material. Each unit—in its three or four readings—provides a total of between about 9,000 and 11,000 words of text, not counting references or exercises. The main point is for students to **read.** Although many classes will seek additional material externally, a class that adopts MAR can be assured of having plenty to work with.

Almost every reading is taken, in minimally adapted form, from a book or academic/professional journal. Two introductory passages (in

Unit 1 and Unit 3) have been composed expressly for this book in order to provide narrowly focused background material. Beyond these pieces, readers are in the hands of "real-world" authors and their difficult, lexically diffuse, and allusion-filled creations. Journal articles and book excerpts predominate, but MAR offers (in Unit 2) a book review and a government pamphlet as well. Academic classes in English-medium universities often draw on materials in such "fringe" genres, so EAP students deserve a chance to work with them as well.

Footnotes and endnotes have been preserved. No one is likely to read these for general enlightenment, but they are part of academic literature. EAP readers need to work with them, if only to get good at ignoring them when appropriate. Although MAR is not meant as a writing book, some tasks do involve writing from external sources, which raises a need to compose reference notes according to prescribed formats. The readings in MAR provide models in the APA style. Teachers are, of course, free to require other formats in student writing, but they should provide samples of notes in the format they prefer.

Unit Structure

Each of the four units in MAR provides enough material for approximately 12 to 18 hours of instructional time. Not every teacher will choose to do all the exercises for every reading, so MAR (or at least much of it) could be covered in a term of as few as 10 four-hour weeks. The exercise sections contain activities for integrating information across readings, but these can be skipped if necessary. It is worth remembering, though, that such integration is among the main reading purposes cited by Grabe and Stoller as important in academic reading. We encourage teachers to use these exercises if doing so is practical.

Since one aspect of reading practice builds on others, the units of MAR are laid out in "tiers," not in "sections" (with the segregation that word implies). Each unit has been organized into three tiers. In general, there is one reading per tier, although the first tier in Unit 3 contains two passages (both necessary to provide conceptual background for the other two tiers). Each tier focuses on different aspects of academic reading, and again Grabe and Stoller's analysis has driven the conception of which aspects are vital.

First Tier
Overview or survey passage (ca. 800 words)
Focus: Basic Comprehension

- Text model (main ideas/support, etc.)
- Situational model (integration with personal experience)

Second Tier
Either one core passage (3,500–5,000 words) or two of about 1,600 words each)
Focus: Basic Comprehension and Lexical Access

- Semantic networks
- Inventory vocabulary used in the first- and second-tier readings
- Integration of two readings (exercises about relationships between the two)

Third Tier
Core passage (3,500–5,000 words)
Focus: Reading to Learn, Reading to Integrate Information, and Reading to Write a Longer Text Model

- Field model (integrate learning in three readings; discern reliable sources and other topics to pursue in order to learn more)
- Update lexical inventory

We hope that students and teachers enjoy working with the readings in MAR. They represent the work of fine academicians and popular writers. They range widely through topics in science and social observation, but all articles have been chosen with an eye toward enduring substance. Every reading ages. We hope these will age well and will lead to lifelong engagement with academic texts.

UNIT 1

Species

This unit explores ways in which human beings—the species *Homo sapiens*—have affected the development of other animals and plants. The unit is organized as follows:

- FIRST TIER: An Introduction
  Introductory passage: **Humanity's Companion Species**

- SECOND TIER: Potatoes and People
  Book chapter: **The Botany of Desire: The Potato**
  by Michael Pollan

- THIRD TIER: Foxes and Dogs
  Journal article: **Early Canid Domestication: The Farm Fox Experiment**
  by Lyudmila Trut

First Tier: An Introduction

Pre-Reading

DISCUSSION

This reading discusses the role of humans in the evolution of some plants and animals. Before you read, discuss the questions in a small group. Use a dictionary and other reference sources as necessary.

1. Bees need flowers and flowers need bees. List some other examples of how species need each other.

2. List some similarities between dogs and wolves. List some differences.

3. Do you think that humans could have caused wolves to evolve into dogs? If so, how?

Reading

Humanity's Companion Species

1 Life is, very obviously, interdependent. Down to the level of the single cell, one species needs another—or, more likely, many others—for food, shade, protection, even entertainment. Bees need flowers, and flowers need bees. Coral polyps may be small things, but the grand reefs they build make life possible for hundreds of other species, from bacteria to sharks. If coral goes extinct, so may they. Something similar could be said for the entire ecosystems that hum around the Asian elephant, the baobab tree, or the human.

2 The far-reaching role of humans in the evolution of some plants is eloquently described by Michael Pollan in his landmark book *The Botany of Desire*. Thinking of domesticated crops like apples and potatoes, he remarks, "We automatically think of domestication as something we do to other species, but it makes just as much sense to think of it as something certain plants and animals have done to us, a clever evolutionary strategy for advancing their own interests. The species that have spent the last ten thousand or so years figuring out how best to feed, heal, clothe, intoxicate, and otherwise delight us have made themselves some of nature's greatest success stories."[1]

---

[1] From *The Botany of Desire: A Plant's Eye View of the World* by M. Pollan, 2001.

3 The time period Pollan mentions is a rough approximation of the span during which settled agricultural life has been common. His focus on plants has made him too conservative, perhaps by a few thousand years. One grave in the Middle East contains the bones of a pup—either a dog or a wolf—buried along with a human about 14,000 years ago. A skeleton that is distinctively from a dog, not a wolf, was discovered in a Middle Eastern cave and dated by archaeologists to about 12,000 years ago. Both of these dates precede the point at which other companion species, such as sheep or cattle, probably became adjunct to human communities (more in line with Pollan's 10,000 years). Horses probably did not get domesticated until some 4,500 years ago. The evidence, then, points to the dog as the first species to employ Pollan's "clever evolutionary strategy" of systematically conforming to human wishes.

4 Speculation as to exactly how that happened remains lively, partly because reliable evidence allows for several credible scenarios. Almost no one doubts that domesticated dogs, the species known as *Canis familiaris*, descended from the wolf, *Canis lupus*. A longstanding belief held that dogs diverged from the wolf line as a result of artificial selection by humans. Or, more accurately, natural selection along Darwinian lines was redirected as the wishes of humans became a factor in determining which organisms were the "fittest" in certain environmental niches. This scenario places humans in the driver's seat, choosing to welcome certain docile wolves and breeding them selectively until they were different enough from wild wolves to constitute a new species.

5 It is also possible that this divergence happened in response to canine initiative, not human. For example, those individual wolves that neither ran away nor attacked at the sight of humans may have been tolerated as they ate garbage tossed out at the margins of human camps. This would confer a great survival advantage by securing a relatively constant and easy-to-get supply of food. These human-compatible individuals mated and had pups that grew up able to co-exist with humans, and the development of a companion species was underway. This scenario is bolstered by DNA analyses, which have found a one percent difference between the genome (basic genetic structure) of dogs and that of wolves. According to standard formulas regarding the rate of genetic change, the wolf-dog separation point would then be between 100,000 and 135,000 years ago. At such an early point, any human societies were probably like hunting packs themselves and were probably too rudimentary to undertake the deliberate domestication of any animal, even one as well-suited to it as the wolf-dog. A more accidental cozying-up between the two species is a lot easier to believe at that stage in human development.

6 Still, strong evidence from unique experiments in Siberia suggests that the human-dog connection could have been formed on a much shorter time scale, regardless of what the DNA analyses say. The late Dmitry Bulyaev began a series of breeding experiments in the 1950s that, over the course of a mere 40 years, achieved remarkable results. He worked with silver foxes, a close relative of wolves and dogs, captured in the wild and then housed at his research facility in Novosibirsk. This experiment is described in detail by Lyudmila Trut later in this unit. The long and short of it is that it shows how a population of canids can be dramatically transformed in a very short time simply by selecting for the trait of tameness. It further suggests that extremely small genetic shifts, far smaller than one percent of the total genome, may be enough to nudge a wild species into the fold of human companions.

Post-Reading

Basic Comprehension

SHORT ANSWER

Answer the questions in your own words.

1. Paragraph 2 contains a long quote from Michael Pollan. What is Pollan's main point?

_____

_____

_____

2. What evidence suggests that the separation of wolves and dogs into two species was not caused entirely by artificial selection?

_____

_____

_____

3. What kind of experiments did Dmitry Bulyaev conduct?

_____

_____

_____

MATCHING

Complete each sentence with the best number from the box. One number will be used twice.

4,500	10,000	12,000	14,000	100,000–135,000

1. A fossil that shows dogs and wolves had become noticeably different is about _____ years old.
2. A fossil that suggests humans and wolves or dogs lived together is about _____ years old.
3. DNA analyses suggest dogs and wolves began to separate as species _____ years ago.
4. Horses began to be domesticated about _____ years ago.
5. Humans began to live together with some farm animals about _____ years ago.
6. Plants began to be domesticated about _____ years ago.

Vocabulary

MULTIPLE CHOICE

Choose the word or phrase closest in meaning to each italicized word.

1. "Thinking of *domesticated* crops like apples and potatoes, he remarks. . . ."
   a. adapted for human use
   b. common
   c. different from each other
   d. nutritious

2. "The time period Pollan mentions is a *rough* approximation of the span during which settled agricultural life has been common."
   a. amazing
   b. not exact
   c. simple
   d. very long

3. "A skeleton that is *distinctively* from a dog, not a wolf, was discovered in a Middle Eastern cave and dated by archaeologists to about 12,000 years ago."
   a. easily identified as
   b. probably
   c. thought to be
   d. unusually

4. "Still, strong evidence from *unique* experiments in Siberia suggests that the human-dog connection could have been formed on a much shorter time scale, regardless of what the DNA analyses say."
   a. detailed
   b. long-running
   c. overlooked
   d. one-of-a-kind

PARAPHRASING

Restate each numbered sentence in the paragraphs using the word in parentheses. Refer to a dictionary if necessary.

① (speculation) In the twentieth century, archaeologists gave much thought to the question of how domestication of plant species began. ② (speculated) Because domestication of plants occurred around the same time in different parts of the world, some hypothesized that global climate played a role. ③ (speculative) Although global climate seems almost certain to have played some role, scientists remained uncertain of the exact mechanism by which climate affected domestication. Archaeologists also debated where domestication took place. ④ (speculated) Some theorists suggested that agriculture began in areas where plant species such as wild wheat were plentiful. However, other research showed that agriculture may have begun near the edges of the species' habitat rather than near the center. ⑤ (divergence) No matter exactly where and how plant species were first domesticated, as domestication progressed, differences between traits of the domesticated species and its wild relative emerged. ⑥ (diverged) There are several ways domesticated wheat has become different from wild wheat: it stays on its stalk longer when it is ripe, it has thinner husks, and each plant produces many more seeds. ⑦ (divergence) Early agricultural practices likely encouraged the separation between wild and domesticated wheat. ⑧ (divergent) Early agriculturalists may have selected mutant plants with the new traits and intentionally or unintentionally provided a situation more favorable to their growth than to that of plants with wild traits.

1. _____

   _____

2. _____

   _____

3. _____

   _____

4. _____

   _____

5. _____

   _____

6. _____

   _____

7. _____

   _____

8. _____

   _____

Reading Focus

Grouping Information

Grouping information can help readers understand the material. Grouped material is also easier to remember because it is logical and consistent.

CATEGORIZING

Arrange these events into three groups. Which of the events do you think were **unintentional**? Which were **deliberate**? Which were probably a combination of the two? Discuss your answers in a small group. <u>Optional</u>: Try adding two other events (from your own knowledge of human development) to each group.

development of agriculture   invention of the airplane
development of writing   invention of the wheel
discovery of penicillin   use of fire
domestication of the dog

Unintentional	Deliberate	Combination

Second Tier: Potatoes and People

Pre-Reading

DISCUSSION

This reading deals with genetically modified food crops. Before you read, discuss the questions in a small group. Use a dictionary and other reference sources as necessary.

1. Distinguish between the members of each pair given.

   Example: plant / crop

   "Plant" is a more general word, meaning any kind of vegetation. It could be wild or it could be deliberately grown on a farm. A "crop" is a type of plant that humans grow so they can gather all or parts of it for some specific use (for food, fuel, fiber, etc.).

   a. genetically modified species / hybrid species
   b. species / individual
   c. species / variety

2. How do you think genetically modified crops differ from traditional crops?

Reading

The Botany of Desire: The Potato

1 For nature as much as for people, the garden has always been a place to experiment, to try out new hybrids and mutations. Species that never cross in the wild will freely hybridize on land cleared by people. That's because a novel hybrid has a hard time finding a purchase in the tight weave of an established meadow or forest ecosystem; every possible niche is apt to be already filled. But a garden—or a roadside or a dump heap— is by comparison an "open" habitat in which a new hybrid has a much better shot, and if it happens to catch our fancy, to gratify a human desire, it stands to make its way in the world. One theory of the origins of agriculture holds that domesticated plants first emerged on dump heaps, where the discarded seeds of the wild plants that people gathered and ate— already unconsciously selected for sweetness or size or power—took root,

flourished, and eventually hybridized. In time people gave the best of these hybrids a place in the garden, and there, together, the people and the plants embarked on a series of experiments in coevolution that would change them both forever. . . .

2 It is only by trial and error that my garden ever improves, so I continue to experiment. Recently I planted something new—something very new, as a matter of fact—and embarked on my most ambitious experiment to date. I planted a potato called "NewLeaf" that has been genetically engineered (by the Monsanto corporation) to produce its own insecticide. This it does in every cell of every leaf, stem, flower, root, and—this is the unsettling part—every spud.

3 The scourge of potatoes has always been the Colorado potato beetle, a handsome, voracious insect that can pick a plant clean of its leaves virtually overnight, starving the tubers in the process. Supposedly, any Colorado potato beetle that takes so much as a nibble of a NewLeaf leaf is doomed, its digestive tract pulped, in effect, by the bacterial toxin manufactured in every part of these plants.

4 I wasn't at all sure I really *wanted* the NewLeaf potatoes I'd be digging at the end of the season. In this respect my experiment in growing them was very different from anything else I've ever done in my garden— whether growing apples or tulips or [anything else]. All of those I'd planted because I really wanted what the plants promised. What I wanted here was to gratify not so much a desire as a curiosity: Do they work? Are these genetically modified potatoes a good idea, either to plant or to eat? If not mine, then whose desire *do* they gratify? And finally, what might they have to tell us about the future of the relationship between plants and people? To answer these questions, or at least begin to, would take more than the tools of the gardener (or the eater); I'd need as well the tools of the journalist, without which I couldn't hope to enter the world from which these potatoes had come. So you could say there was something fundamentally artificial about my experiment in growing NewLeaf potatoes. But then, artificiality seems very much to the point.

5 Certainly my NewLeafs are aptly named. They're part of a new class of crop plant that is transforming the long, complex, and by now largely invisible food chain that links everyone of us to the land. By the time I conducted my experiment, more than fifty million acres of American farmland had already been planted to genetically modified crops, most of it corn, soybeans, cotton, and potatoes that have been engineered either to produce their own pesticide or to withstand herbicides. The not-so-distant future will, we're told, bring us potatoes genetically modified to absorb less fat when fried, corn that can withstand drought, lawns that don't ever have to be mowed, "golden rice" rich in Vitamin A, bananas and potatoes

that deliver vaccines, tomatoes enhanced with flounder genes (to withstand frost), and cotton that grows in every color of the rainbow.

6 It's probably not too much to say that this new technology represents the biggest change in the terms of our relationship with plants since people first learned how to cross one plant with another. With genetic engineering, human control of nature is taking a giant step forward. The kind of reordering of nature represented by the rows in a farmer's field can now take place at a whole new level: within the genome of the plants themselves. Truly, we have stepped out onto new ground.

7 Or have we?

8 Just how novel these plants really are is in fact one of the biggest questions about them, and the companies that have developed them give contradictory answers. The industry simultaneously depicts these plants as the linchpins of a biological revolution, part of a "paradigm shift" that will make agriculture more sustainable and feed the world—and, oddly enough, as the same old spuds, corn, and soybeans, at least so far as those of us at the eating end of the food chain should be concerned. The new plants are novel enough to be patented, yet not so novel as to warrant a label telling us what it is we're eating. It would seem they are chimeras: "revolutionary" in the patent office and on the farm, "nothing new" in the supermarket and the environment. . . .

9 Here at the planter's end of the food chain, where I began my experiment after Monsanto agreed to let me test-drive its NewLeafs, things certainly look new and different. After digging two shallow trenches in my vegetable garden and lining them with compost, I untied the purple mesh bag of seed potatoes Monsanto had sent and opened the grower's guide tied around its neck. Potatoes, you will recall from kindergarten experiments, are grown not from actual seeds but from the eyes of other potatoes, and the dusty, stone-colored chunks of tuber I carefully laid at the bottom of the trench looked much like any other. Yet the grower's guide that comes with them put me in mind not so much of planting vegetables as booting up a new software release.

10 By "opening and using this product," the card informed me, I was now "licensed" to grow these potatoes, but only for a single generation; the crop I would water and tend and harvest was mine, yet also not mine. That is, the potatoes I would dig come September would be mine to eat or sell, but their genes would remain the intellectual property of Monsanto, protected under several U.S. patents, including 5,196,525; 5,164,316; 5,322,938; and 5,352,605. Were I to save even one of these spuds to plant next year—something I've routinely done with my potatoes in the past—I would be breaking federal law. (I had to wonder, what would be the legal status of any "volunteers"—those plants that, with no prompting from the

gardener, sprout each spring from tubers overlooked during the previous harvest?) The small print on the label also brought the disconcerting news that my potato plants were *themselves* registered as a pesticide with the Environmental Protection Administration (U.S. EPA Reg. No. 524–474).

11 If proof were needed that the food chain that begins with seeds and ends on our dinner plates is in the midst of revolutionary change, the small print that accompanied my NewLeafs will do. That food chain has been unrivaled for its productivity: on average, an American farmer today grows enough food each year to feed a hundred people. Yet that achievement—that power over Nature—has come at a price. The modern industrial farmer cannot grow that much food without large quantities of chemical fertilizers, pesticides, machines, and fuel. This expensive set of "inputs," as they're called, saddles the farmer with debt, jeopardizes his health, erodes his soil and ruins its fertility, pollutes the groundwater, and compromises the safety of the food we eat. Thus the gain in the farmer's power has been trailed by a host of new vulnerabilities.

12 All this I'd heard before, of course—but always from environmentalists or organic farmers. What is new is to hear the same critique from industrial farmers, government officials, and the agribusiness companies that sold farmers on all those expensive inputs in the first place. Taking a page from Wendell Berry, of all people, Monsanto declared in a recent annual report that "current agricultural technology is unsustainable."

13 What is to rescue the American food chain is a new kind of plant. Genetic engineering promises to replace expensive and toxic chemicals with expensive but apparently benign genetic information: crops that, like my NewLeafs, can protect themselves from insects and diseases without the help of pesticides. In the case of the NewLeaf, a gene borrowed from one strain of a common bacterium found in the soil—Bacillus *thuringiensis*, or "Bt" for short—gives the potato plant's cells the information they need to manufacture a toxin lethal to the Colorado potato beetle. This gene is now Monsanto's intellectual property. With genetic engineering, agriculture has entered the information age, and Monsanto's aim, it would appear, is to become its Microsoft—supplying the proprietary "operating systems"—the metaphor is theirs—to run this new generation of plants.

14 The metaphors we use to describe the natural world strongly influence the way we approach it, the style and extent of our attempts at control. It makes all the difference in (and to) the world if one conceives of a farm as a factory or a forest as a farm. Now we're about to find out what happens when people begin approaching the genes of our food plants as software.

Andean Origins

15 The patented potatoes I was planting are descended from wild ancestors growing on the Andean altiplano, the potato's "center of diversity." It was here that *Solanum tuberosum* was first domesticated more than seven thousand years ago by ancestors of the Incas. Actually, some of the potatoes in my garden are closely related to those ancient potatoes. Among the half dozen or so different varieties I grow are a couple of ancient heirlooms, including the Peruvian blue potato. This starchy spud is about the size of a golf ball; when you slice it through the middle the flesh looks as though it has been tie-dyed the most gorgeous shade of blue. . . .

16 Since the margins and hedgerows of the Andean farm were, and still are, populated by weedy wild potatoes, the farmer's cultivated varieties have regularly crossed with their wild relatives, in the process refreshing the gene pool and producing new hybrids. Whenever one of these new potatoes proves its worth—surviving a drought or storm, say, or winning praise at the dinner table—it is promoted from the margins to the fields and, in time, to the neighbors' fields as well. Artificial selection is thus a continual local process, each new potato the product of an ongoing back-and-forth between the land and its cultivators, mediated by the universe of all possible potatoes: the species' genome.

17 The genetic diversity cultivated by the Incas and their descendants is an extraordinary cultural achievement and a gift of incalculable value to the rest of the world. A free and unencumbered gift, one might add, quite unlike my patented and trademarked NewLeafs. "Intellectual property" is a recent, Western concept that means nothing to a Peruvian farmer, then or now.[1] Of course, Francisco Pizarro was looking for neither plants nor intellectual property when he conquered the Incas; he had eyes only for gold. None of the conquistadores could have imagined it, but the funny-looking tubers they encountered high in the Andes would prove to be the single most important treasure they would bring back from the New World. . . .

18 All domesticated plants are in some sense artificial, living archives of both cultural and natural information that people have helped to "design." Any given type of potato reflects the human desires that have been bred into it. One that's been selected to yield long, handsome french fries or unblemished, round potato chips is the expression of a national food chain and a culture that likes its potatoes highly processed. At the

---

[1] In fact, "intellectual property" has been defined under recent trade agreements in such a way as to specifically exclude any innovations that are not the private, marketable property of an individual or corporation. Thus a corporation's new potato qualifies as intellectual property, but not a tribe's.

same time, some of the more delicate European fingerlings growing beside my NewLeafs imply an economy of small-market growers and a cultural taste for eating potatoes fresh—for none of these varieties can endure much travel or time in storage. I'm not sure exactly what cultural values to ascribe to my Peruvian blues; perhaps nothing more than a craving for variety among a people who ate potatoes morning, noon, and night.

19 "Tell me what you eat," Anthelme Brillat-Savarin famously claimed, and "I will tell you what you are." The qualities of a potato—as of any domesticated plant or animal—are a fair reflection of the values of the people who grow and eat it. Yet all these qualities already existed in the potato, somewhere within the universe of genetic possibilities presented by the species *Solanum tuberosum*. And though that universe may be vast, it is not infinite. Since unrelated species in nature cannot be crossed, the breeder's art has always run up against a natural limit of what a potato is willing, or able, to do—that species' essential identity. Nature has always exercised a kind of veto over what culture can do with a potato.

20 Until now. The NewLeaf is the first potato to override that veto. Monsanto likes to depict genetic engineering as just one more chapter in the ancient history of human modifications of nature, a story going back to the discovery of fermentation. The company defines the word *biotechnology* so broadly as to take in the brewing of beer, cheese making, and selective breeding: all are "technologies" that involve the manipulation of life-forms.

21 This new biotechnology has overthrown the old rules governing the relationship of nature and culture in a plant. Domestication has never been a simple one-way process in which our species has controlled others; other species participate only so far as their interests are served, and many plants (such as the oak) simply sit the whole game out. That game is the one Darwin called "artificial selection:" and its rules have never been any different from the rules that govern natural selection. The plant in its wildness proposes new qualities, and then man (or, in the case of natural selection, nature) selects which of those qualities will survive and prosper. But about one rule Darwin was emphatic; as he wrote in *The Origin of Species*, "Man does not actually produce variability."

22 Now he does. For the first time, breeders can bring qualities at will from anywhere in nature into the genome of a plant: from fireflies (the quality of luminescence), from flounders (frost tolerance), from viruses (disease resistance), and, in the case of my potatoes, from the soil bacterium known as *Bacillus thuringiensis*. Never in a million years of natural or artificial selection would these species have proposed those qualities. "Modification by descent" has been replaced by . . . something else.

23 Now, it is true that genes occasionally move between species; the genome of many species appears to be somewhat more fluid than scientists used to think. Yet for reasons we don't completely understand, distinct species do exist in nature, and they exhibit a certain genetic integrity—sex between them, when it does occur, doesn't produce fertile offspring. Nature presumably has some reason for erecting these walls, even if they are permeable on occasion. Perhaps, as some biologists believe, the purpose of keeping species separate is to put barriers in the path of pathogens, to contain their damage so that a single germ can't wipe out life on Earth in a stroke.

24 The deliberate introduction into a plant of genes transported not only across species but across whole phyla means that the wall of that plant's essential identity—its irreducible wildness, you might say—has been breached, not by a virus, as sometimes happens in nature, but by humans wielding powerful new tools. . . .

25 What is perhaps most striking about the NewLeafs coming up in my garden is the added human intelligence that the insertion of the *Bacillus thuringiensis* gene represents. In the past that intelligence resided outside the plant, in the minds of the organic farmers and gardeners (myself included) who used Bt, commonly in the form of a spray, to manipulate the ecological relationship between certain insects and a certain bacterium in order to foil those insects. One way to look at genetic engineering is that it allows a larger portion of human culture and intelligence to be incorporated into the plants themselves. From this perspective, my NewLeafs are just plain smarter than the rest of my potatoes. The others will depend on my knowledge and experience when the Colorado potato beetles strike. The NewLeafs, already knowing what I know about bugs and Bt, will take care of themselves. So while my genetically engineered plants might at first seem like alien beings, that's not quite right; they're more like us than other plants because there is more of us in them. . . .

26 My NewLeafs are clones of clones of plants that were first engineered more than a decade ago in a long, low-slung brick building on the bank of the Missouri that would look like any other corporate complex if not for its stunning roofline. What appear from a distance to be shimmering crenellations of glass turn out to be the twenty-six greenhouses that crown the building in a dramatic sequence of triangular peaks. The first generation of genetically altered plants—of which the NewLeaf potato is one—has been grown under this roof, in these greenhouses, since 1984. Especially in the early days of biotechnology, no one knew for sure if it was safe to grow these plants outdoors, in nature. Today this research and development facility is one of a small handful of such places—Monsanto has only two or three competitors in the world—where the world's crop plants are being redesigned.

27 Dave Starck, one of Monsanto's senior potato people, escorted me through the clean rooms where potatoes are genetically engineered. He explained that there are two ways of splicing foreign genes into a plant— by infecting it with agrobacterium, a pathogen whose modus operandi is to break into a plant cell's nucleus and replace its DNA with some of its own, or by shooting it with a gene gun. For reasons not yet understood, the agrobacterium method seems to work best on broadleaf species such as the potato, the gene gun better on grasses, such as corn and wheat. The gene gun is a strangely high-low piece of technology, but the main thing you need to know about it is that the gun here is not a metaphor: a .22 shell is used to fire stainless-steel projectiles dipped in a DNA solution at a stem or leaf of the target plant. If all goes well, some of the DNA will pierce the wall of some of the cells' nuclei and elbow its way into the double helix: a bully breaking into a line dance. If the new DNA happens to land in the right place—and no one yet knows what, or where, that place is—the plant grown from that cell will express the new gene. *That's it?*

28 That's it.

29 Apart from its slightly more debonair means of entry, the agrobacterium works in much the same way. In the clean rooms, where the air pressure is kept artificially high to prevent errant microbes from wandering in, technicians sit at lab benches before petri dishes in which fingernail-sized sections of potato stem have been placed in a clear nutrient jelly. Into this medium they squirt a solution of agrobacteria, which have already had their genes swapped with the ones Monsanto wants to insert (specific enzymes can be used to cut and paste precise sequences of DNA). In addition to the Bt gene being spliced, a "marker" gene is also included—typically this is a gene conferring resistance to a specific antibiotic. This way, the technicians can later flood the dish with the antibiotic to *see* which cells have taken up the new DNA; any that haven't simply die. The marker gene can also serve as a kind of DNA fingerprint, allowing Monsanto to identify its plants and their descendants long after they've left the lab. By performing a simple test on any potato leaf in my garden, a Monsanto agent can prove whether or not the plant is the company's intellectual property. I realized that, whatever else it is, genetic engineering is also a powerful technique for transforming plants into private property, by giving everyone of them what amounts to its own Universal Product Code.

Post-Reading

Basic Comprehension

SHORT ANSWER

Answer the questions in your own words.

1. What is the purpose of the genetic modification to the NewLeaf potato?

   _____

   _____

   _____

2. Pollan compares genetically modified crops to computer software. Why do you think he makes this comparison?

   _____

   _____

   _____

3. In Paragraph 20, Pollan states that "Monsanto likes to depict genetic engineering as just one more chapter in the ancient history of human modifications of nature, a story going back to the discovery of fermentation." However, he seems to disagree with this depiction. What does Pollan see as the fundamental difference between genetic modification and the development of hybrids by natural and artificial selection?

   _____

   _____

   _____

MULTIPLE CHOICE

Circle the choice that best answers each question.

1. Which statement is closest to the main idea of the reading?

   a. Developments in genetic modification allow corporations greater control over agriculture.
   b. Genetic modifications enable farmers to produce higher crop yields than is possible using traditional crops.
   c. Genetically modified organisms are harmful because of the toxins they contain.
   d. The varieties of potato that evolved in the Andes are being replaced by a global monoculture.

2. Which statement best describes the attitude Pollan expresses toward genetically modified crops?

   a. mild curiosity about a scientific process
   b. powerful opposition to a harmful change
   c. slight mistrust of an inevitable advance
   d. strong support of an important discovery

3. Which statements describe what Pollan considered artificial about his planting NewLeaf potatoes? (Choose two.)

   a. The potatoes contain artificial genes.
   b. The potatoes don't gratify a desire.
   c. The potatoes require artificial fertilizers.
   d. The potatoes were planted in deliberate rows.

4. According to Paragraph 10, which warnings were included in the grower's guide Pollan received with his NewLeaf potatoes? (Choose two.)

   a. A government agency listed the potato plants a pesticide.
   b. He could not keep and replant the potatoes he grew.
   c. He would be able to eat or sell the potatoes he harvested.
   d. The potatoes might grow back as "volunteers" the next year.

5. According to Paragraphs 11–13, what problem in modern agriculture does genetic engineering seek to solve?

   a. decreasing productivity on American farms
   b. plant diseases caused by *Bacillus thuringiensis* infections
   c. rising food and seed prices
   d. unsustainability of farming using vast amounts of inputs

6. Why is there such a wide variety of Andean potatoes?

   a. Ancestors of the Incas, unlike other early farmers, valued diversity of species.
   b. Domesticated potatoes regularly cross with wild potatoes on the Andean antiplano.
   c. The farmers continually crossed their plants to produce new types.
   d. The potatoes on the Andean antiplano had been collected from various different areas.

7. What does Paragraph 18 suggest about the type of potato that "yields long, handsome french fries or unblemished, round potato chips"?

   a. They are difficult to grow.
   b. They are unrelated to European fingerlings.
   c. They can be stored a long time.
   d. They have been genetically modified.

8. Which statement best expresses the most important limitation farmers faced in cross-breeding potatoes prior to genetic engineering technology?

   a. It took a long time to produce hybrids with desired traits.
   b. The potato species contained few genetic possibilities for different traits.
   c. They could breed for traits a species possessed but not for traits from other species.
   d. They had to obtain intellectual property permission to use varieties developed by other farmers.

9. According to Paragraph 21, what characterizes natural and artificial selection in the process of domestication?

   a. Artificial selection generally serves human interests but natural selection generally doesn't.
   b. Natural selection acts only in wild species and artificial selection only in domesticated species.
   c. They both involve one-way processes of a species controlling another.
   d. They both select for features found in nature but neither produces new qualities.

10. What can be inferred from Paragraph 23 about what some biologists believe?

   a. If different species could exchange genes easily, all species would be more vulnerable to disease.

   b. Life on Earth is likely to be eliminated by a single germ someday.

   c. Additional legal barriers are needed to keep species separate because of the danger pathogens pose.

   d. Genes are never transmitted between different species in nature.

11. According to Paragraph 25, why are Pollan's NewLeafs "just plain smarter than the rest of [his] potatoes"?

   a. The "knowledge" that Bt will protect them is built into them.

   b. They have a larger amount of genetic information than other potatoes.

   c. Genetic engineers inserted human DNA into them.

   d. Farmers save time and money, making NewLeafs a wise choice.

12. According to Paragraph 29, which statement is NOT a result of inserting marker genes into plants?

   a. Plant varieties become private property.

   b. Researchers are able to determine which cells contain the modified genes.

   c. Company representatives can figure out what plants contain their genes.

   d. The plants develop a resistance to certain bacteria.

Vocabulary

MULTIPLE CHOICE

Choose the word or phrase closest in meaning to each italicized word in the sentences from the reading.

1. "Thus the gain in the farmer's power has been trailed by a host of new *vulnerabilities*."
   a. needs
   b. promises
   c. responsibilities
   d. weaknesses

2. "Nature presumably has some reason for *erecting* these walls, even if they are permeable on occasion."
   a. changing
   b. building
   c. selecting
   d. wanting

3. "Nature presumably has some reason for erecting these walls, even if they are *permeable* on occasion."
   a. falling apart
   b. difficult to understand fully
   c. penetrable; have holes that allow things through
   d. maintained artificially

4. "The deliberate introduction into a plant of genes transported not only across species but across whole phyla means that the wall of that plant's essential identity—its irreducible wildness, you might say—has been *breached*, not by a virus, as sometimes happens in nature, but by humans wielding powerful new tools."
   a. broken through
   b. erased
   c. made unhealthy
   d. reduced

5. "Apart from its slightly more *debonair* means of entry, the agrobacterium works in much the same way."

   a. calm
   b. controlled
   c. natural
   d. sophisticated

6. "In the clean rooms, where the air pressure is kept artificially high to prevent *errant* microbes from wandering in, technicians sit at lab benches before petri dishes in which fingernail-sized sections of potato stem have been placed in a clear nutrient jelly."

   a. disease-causing
   b. different
   c. aimlessly moving
   d. numerous

PARAPHRASING

Use the best vocabulary item from the list to rephrase each statement. Change as much of the original as necessary to use the item you have chosen, but do not change the meaning of the original. Use each item from the list only once.

Vocabulary Items

ancestors	deliberate (adj.)	subsist
commodity	intractable/intractability	succumbed
cultivate	modify	vulnerable

1. Researchers have managed to change the genetic code of crops so that patented varieties are sterile.

   _____

   _____

2. The price of products bought and sold on the market like corn or pork determines the profitability of farmers' yields.

   _____

   _____

3. The progenitors of modern potatoes were harvested in the Andes.

   _____

   _____

4. Unlike natural selection, artificial selection occurs when humans make an intentional choice of one trait over another and help individuals with that trait to thrive.

   _____

   _____

5. In spite of the thousands of years' experience humans have with agriculture, nature remains difficult to control.

   _____

   _____

6. Pollan describes his attempt to grow and care for genetically modified potatoes.

   _____

   _____

Reading Focus

Polysemy ("Many meanings")

Dictionaries often list several definitions for a word. Sometimes the different meanings of homonyms (words that have the same sound and spelling, but have different meanings) are so distinct that it is easy to tell which definition is intended by the author. For example, you probably know whether the word *right* means "in accordance with the facts" or "the opposite of left." However, it might be more difficult to determine whether it means "in conformity with the facts" or "in accordance with what is proper." Even more difficult might be the distinction between "in accordance with what is proper" and "tending to do what is good." Still, the distinction is important to accurate reading.

MULTIPLE CHOICE

In this activity, many of the options are accurate definitions for the word they follow. However, only one conforms to the intended meaning of the word in the reading (see paragraph numbers). Choose the definition that best defines the word as it is used in the reading.

1. *compromises* (Paragraph 11)
   a. causes danger
   b. finds a solution between two extremes
   c. provides a harmful thing
   d. gives in so an agreement can be reached

2. *host* (Paragraph 11)
   a. organism that a parasite lives on
   b. person who has invited guests
   c. person who leads a TV show or event
   d. very large number

3. *descended from* (Paragraph 15)
   a. act less dignified than expected of one's position
   b. in a logical progression
   c. come from an older version
   d. go from a higher place to a lower one

4. *yield* (Paragraph 18)
   a. break under pressure
   b. give over control of
   c. give way
   d. produce

Building a Text Model

PART 1: ORGANIZATIONAL TECHNIQUE

SHORT ANSWER

Answer the questions about the reading.

1. Authors use various techniques and combinations of techniques to present and support their points. Which of the following best describes the organization of the actual passage?

   a. alternating between analysis (scientific, economic, and historical) and personal narrative

   b. arguing about use of genetically engineered products through the presentation of advantages and disadvantages

   c. chronologically describing advances in evolution and biological science

   d. presenting a thesis followed by historical and scientific data in support of the thesis

2. What advantages and disadvantages does this organizational technique present as far as the reader is concerned? In your answer, consider such factors as the ease and difficulty of processing information, maintaining interest in the topic, and overall comprehension.

   _____

   _____

   _____

PART 2: PARAGRAPH ORGANIZATION

COMPLETION

Next to each set of paragraph numbers, list the organizational descriptor that best applies. Then list the main idea of those paragraphs. The first two have been done for you as examples.

Paragraph Number(s)	Organizational Descriptor	Main Idea
1	historical/ scientific analysis	Hybrid plants have developed through a process of coevolution with humans.
2–4	personal narrative	Genetically modified potatoes can produce their own insecticides, but Pollan has questions about their safety and desirability.
5–8		
9–10		
11–14		
15–19		

20–25		
26		
27–28		
29		

Putting Reading to Work

WRITING

Michael Pollan indirectly raises two questions. Do some research on ONE of these questions. Use one or two reference sources outside this chapter to gather information about the environmental situation in that country. You may use print or online sources. Present your findings in a one- or two-page paper or in a short three-to-five-minute oral presentation.

1. Can genetic modification reduce the environmentally harmful inputs needed for modern farming?

2. What effects will result from the growing corporate control over agriculture?

Third Tier: Foxes and Dogs

Pre-Reading

DISCUSSION

This reading by Lyudmila Trut is mentioned in Tier 1. It describes some experiments involving foxes. From these experiments, the researchers drew conclusions about dogs. Before you read, discuss the questions in a small group. After you read, see which of your predictions were correct.

1. What are possible reasons why the scientists studying the domestication of dogs chose to experiment on foxes rather than wolves?

2. How do you think they might have conducted their experiment?

3. What questions do you think their experiment might have answered?

Reading

Early Canid Domestication: The Farm Fox Experiment

1 Foxes bred for tamability in a 40-year experiment exhibit remarkable transformations that suggest an interplay between behavioral genetics and development. When scientists ponder how animals came to be domesticated, they almost inevitably wind up thinking about dogs. The dog was probably the first domestic animal, and it is the one in which domestication has progressed the furthest—far enough to turn *Canis lupus* into *Canis familiaris*. Evolutionary theorists have long speculated about exactly how dogs' association with human beings may have been linked to their divergence from their wild wolf forebears, a topic that anthropologist Darcy Morey has discussed in some detail. As Morey pointed out, debates about the origins of animal domestication tend to focus on "the issue of intentionality"—the extent to which domestication was the result of deliberate human choice. Was domestication actually "self-domestication," the colonization of new ecological niches by animals such as wolves? Or did it result from intentional decisions by human beings? How you answer those questions will determine how you understand the morphological and physiological changes that domestication has brought about—whether as the

results of the pressure of natural selection in a new niche, or as deliberately cultivated advantageous traits. In many ways, though, the question of intentionality is beside the point. Domestication was not a single event but rather a long, complex process. Natural selection and artificial selection may both have operated at different times or even at the same time. For example, even if prehistoric people deliberately set out to domesticate wolves, natural selection would still have been at work. The selective regime may have changed drastically when wolves started living with people, but selective pressure continued regardless of anything Homo sapiens chose to do.

2 Another problem with the debate over intentionality is that it can overshadow other important questions. For example, in becoming domesticated, animals have undergone a host of changes in morphology, physiology and behavior. What do those changes have in common? Do they stem from a single cause, and if so, what is it? In the case of the dog, Morey identifies one common factor as pedomorphosis, the retention of juvenile traits by adults. Those traits include both morphological ones, such as skulls that are unusually broad for their length, and behavioral ones, such as whining, barking and submissiveness—all characteristics that wolves outgrow but that dogs do not. Morey considers pedomorphosis in dogs a byproduct of natural selection for earlier sexual maturity and smaller body size, features that, according to evolutionary theory, ought to increase the fitness of animals engaged in colonizing a new ecological niche.

3 The common patterns are not confined to a single species. In a wide range of mammals—herbivores and predators, large and small—domestication seems to have brought with it strikingly similar changes in appearance and behavior: changes in size, changes in coat color, even changes in the animals' reproductive cycles. Our research group at the Institute of Cytology and Genetics in Novosibirsk, Siberia, has spent decades investigating such patterns and other questions of the early evolution of domestic animals. Our work grew out of the interests and ideas of the late director of our institute, the geneticist Dmitry K. Belyaev. Like Morey, Belyaev believed that the patterns of changes observed in domesticated animals resulted from genetic changes that occurred in the course of selection. Belyaev, however, believed that the key factor selected for was not size or reproduction, but behavior; specifically amenability to domestication, or tamability. More than any other quality, Belyaev believed, tamability must have determined how well an animal would adapt to life among human beings. Because behavior is rooted in biology, selecting for tameness and against aggression means selecting for physiological changes in the systems that govern

the body's hormones and neuro-chemicals. Those changes, in turn, could have had far-reaching effects on the development of the animals themselves, effects that might well explain why different animals would respond in similar ways when sub-jected to the same kinds of selective pressures.

4 To test his hypothesis, Belyaev decided to turn back the clock to the point at which animals received the first challenge of domestication. By replaying the process, he would be able to see how changes in behav-ior, physiology and morphology first came about. Of course, reproducing the ways and means of those ancient transformations, even in the roughest outlines, would be a for-midable task. To keep things as clear and simple as possible, Belyaev designed a selective-breed-ing program to reproduce a single major factor, a strong selection pressure for tamability. He chose as his experimental model a species taxonomically close to the dog but never before domesticated: *Vulpes vulpes*, the silver fox. Belyaev's fox-breeding experiment occupied the last 26 years of his life. We are carry-ing his work forward. Through genetic selection alone, our research group has created a popu-lation of tame foxes fundamentally different in temperament and behavior from their wild forebears. In the process we have observed some striking changes in physiol-ogy, morphology and behavior, which mirror the changes known in

other domestic animals and bear out many of Belyaev's ideas.

Belyaev's Hypothesis

5 Belyaev began his experiment in 1959, a time when Soviet gen-etics was starting to recover from the anti-Darwinian ideology of Trofim Lysenko. Belyaev's own career had suffered. In 1948, his commitment to orthodox genetics had cost him his job as head of the Department of Fur Animal Breed-ing at the Central Research Labo-ratory of Fur Breeding in Moscow. During the 1950s he continued to conduct genetic research under the guise of studying animal physi-ology. He moved to Novosibirsk, where he helped found the Siber-ian Department of the Soviet (now Russian) Academy of Sciences and became the director of the Depart-ment's Institute of Cytology and Genetics, a post he held from 1959 until his death in 1985. Under his leadership the institute became a center of basic and applied research in both classical genetics and modern molecular genetics. His own work included ground-breaking investigations of evolu-tionary change in animals under extreme conditions (including domestication) and of the evolu-tionary roles of factors such as stress, selection for behavioral traits and the environmental pho-toperiod, or duration of natural daylight. Animal domestication was his lifelong project, and fur bearers were his favorite subjects.

6 Early in the process of domestication, Belyaev noted, most domestic animals had undergone the same basic morphological and physiological changes. Their bodies changed in size and proportions, leading to the appearance of dwarf and giant breeds. The normal pattern of coat color that had evolved as camouflage in the wild altered as well. Many domesticated animals are piebald, completely lacking pigmentation in specific body areas. Hair turned wavy or curly, as it has done in Astrakhan sheep, poodles, domestic donkeys, horses, pigs, goats and even laboratory mice and guinea pigs. Some animals' hair also became longer (Angora type) or shorter (rex type).

7 Tails changed, too. Many breeds of dogs and pigs carry their tails curled up in a circle or semicircle. Some dogs, cats and sheep have short tails resulting from a decrease in the number of tail vertebrae. Ears became floppy. As Darwin noted in Chapter 1 of On the Origin of Species, "not a single domestic animal can be named which has not in some country drooping ears"—a feature not found in any wild animal except the elephant. Another major evolutionary consequence of domestication is loss of the seasonal rhythm of reproduction. Most wild animals in middle latitudes are genetically programmed to mate once a year, during mating seasons cued by changes in daylight. Domestic animals at the same latitudes, however, now can mate and bear young more than once a year and in any season.

8 Belyaev believed that similarity in the patterns of these traits was the result of selection for amenability to domestication. Behavioral responses, he reasoned, are regulated by a fine balance between neurotransmitters and hormones at the level of the whole organism. The genes that control that balance occupy a high level in the hierarchical system of the genome. Even slight alterations in those regulatory genes can give rise to a wide network of changes in the developmental processes they govern. Thus, selecting animals for behavior may lead to other, far-reaching changes in the animals' development. Because mammals from widely different taxonomic groups share similar regulatory mechanisms for hormones and neurochemistry, it is reasonable to believe that selecting them for similar behavior—tameness—should alter those mechanisms, and the developmental pathways they govern, in similar ways.

9 For Belyaev's hypothesis to make evolutionary sense, two more things must be true. Variations in tamability must be determined at least partly by an animal's genes, and domestication must place that animal under strong selective pressure. We have looked into both questions. In the early 1960s our team studied the patterns and

nature of tamability in populations of farm foxes. We cross-bred foxes of different behavior, cross-fostered newborns and even transplanted embryos between donor and host mothers known to react differently to human beings. Our studies showed that about 35 percent of the variations in the foxes' defense response to the experimenter are genetically determined. To get some idea of how powerful the selective pressures on those genes might have been, our group has domesticated other animals, including river otters (*Lutra lutra*) and gray rats (*Rattus norvegicus*) caught in the wild. Out of 50 otters caught during recent years, only eight of them (16 percent) showing weak defensive behavior made a genetic contribution to the next generation. Among the gray rats, only 14 percent of the wild-caught yielded offspring living to adulthood. If our numbers are typical, it is clear that domestication must place wild animals under extreme stress and severe selective pressure.

The Experiment

10 In setting up our breeding experiment, Belyaev bypassed that initial trauma. He began with 30 male foxes and 100 vixens, most of them from a commercial fur farm in Estonia. The founding foxes were already tamer than their wild relatives. Foxes had been farmed since the beginning of this century, so the earliest steps of domestication—capture, caging and isolation from other wild foxes—had already left their marks on our foxes' genes and behavior.

11 From the outset, Belyaev selected foxes for tameness and tameness alone, a criterion we have scrupulously followed. Selection is strict; in recent years, typically not more than 4 or 5 percent of male offspring and about 20 percent of female offspring have been allowed to breed. To ensure that their tameness results from genetic selection, we do not train the foxes. Most of them spend their lives in cages and are allowed only brief "time dosed" contacts with human beings. Pups are caged with their mothers until they are one-half to 2 months old. Then they are caged with their litter mates but without their mothers. At three months, each pup is moved to its own cage.

12 To evaluate the foxes for tameness, we give them a series of tests. When a pup is one month old, an experimenter offers it food from his hand while trying to stroke and handle the pup. The pups are tested twice, once in a cage and once while moving freely with other pups in an enclosure, where they can choose to make contact either with the human experimenter or with another pup. The test is repeated monthly until the pups are six or seven months old.

13 At seven or eight months, when the foxes reach sexual maturity, they are scored for tameness and assigned to one of three classes. The least domesticated

foxes, those that flee from experimenters or bite when stroked or handled, are assigned to Class III. (Even Class III foxes are tamer than the calmest farm-bred foxes. Among other things, they allow themselves to be hand fed.) Foxes in Class II let themselves be petted and handled but show no emotionally friendly response to experimenters. Foxes in Class I are friendly toward experimenters, wagging their tails and whining. In the sixth generation bred for tameness we had to add an even higher-scoring category. Members of Class IE, the "domesticated elite," are eager to establish human contact, whimpering to attract attention and sniffing and licking experimenters like dogs. They start displaying this kind of behavior before they are one month old. By the tenth generation, 18 percent of fox pups were elite; by the 20th, the figure had reached 35 percent. Today elite foxes make up 70 to 80 percent of our experimentally selected population.

14 Now, 40 years and 45,000 foxes after Belyaev began, our experiment has achieved an array of concrete results. The most obvious of them is a unique population of 100 foxes (at latest count), each of them the product of between 30 and 35 generations of selection. They are unusual animals, docile, eager to please and unmistakably domesticated. When tested in groups in an enclosure, pups compete for attention, snarling fiercely at one another as they seek the favor of their human handler. Over the years several of our domesticated foxes have escaped from the fur farm for days. All of them eventually returned. Probably they would have been unable to survive in the wild.

Physical Changes

15 Physically, the foxes differ markedly from their wild relatives. Some of the differences have obvious links to the changes in their social behavior. In dogs, for example, it is well known that the first weeks of life are crucial for forming primary social bonds with human beings. The "window" of bonding opens when a puppy becomes able to sense and explore its surroundings, and it closes when the pup starts to fear unknown stimuli. According to our studies, non-domesticated fox pups start responding to auditory stimuli on day 16 after birth, and their eyes are completely open by day 18 or 19. On average, our domesticated fox pups respond to sounds two days earlier and open their eyes a day earlier than their nondomesticated cousins. Nondomesticated foxes first show the fear response at 6 weeks of age; domesticated ones show it after 9 weeks or even later. (Dogs show it at 8 to 12 weeks, depending on the breed.) As a result, domesticated pups have more time to become incorporated into a human social environment.

16 Moreover, we have found that the delayed development of the fear response is linked to changes in

plasma levels of corticosteroids, hormones concerned with an animal's adaptation to stress. In foxes, the level of corticosteroids rises sharply between the ages of 2 to 4 months and reach adult levels by the age of 8 months. One of our studies found that the more advanced an animal's selection for domesticated behavior was, the later it showed the fear response and the later came the surge in its plasma corticosteroids. Thus, selection for domestication gives rises to changes in the timing of the postnatal development of certain physiological and hormonal mechanisms underlying the formation of social behavior.

17 Other physical changes mirror those in dogs and other domesticated animals. In our foxes, novel traits began to appear in the eighth to tenth selected generations. The first ones we noted were changes in the foxes' coat color, chiefly a loss of pigment in certain areas of the body, leading in some cases to a star-shaped pattern on the face similar to that seen in some breeds of dog. Next came traits such as floppy ears and rolled tails similar to those in some breeds of dog. After 15 to 20 generations we noted the appearance of foxes with shorter tails and legs and with underbites or overbites. The novel traits are still fairly rare. Most of them show up in no more than a few animals per 100 to a few per 10,000. Some have been seen in commercial populations, though at levels at least a magnitude lower than we recorded in our domesticated foxes.

Alternative Explanations

18 What might have caused these changes in the fox population? Before discussing Belyaev's explanation, we should consider other possibilities. Might rates and patterns of changes observed in foxes be due, for example, to inbreeding? That could be true if enough foxes in Belyaev's founding population carried a recessive mutant gene from the trait along with a dominant normal gene that masked its effects. Such mixed-gene, or heterozygous, foxes would have been hidden carriers, unaffected by the mutation themselves but capable of passing it on to later generations.

19 As Morey pointed out, inbreeding might well have been rampant during the early steps of dog domestication. But it certainly cannot explain the novel traits we have observed in our foxes, for two reasons. First, we designed the mating system for our experimental fox population to prevent it. Through outbreeding with foxes from commercial fox farms and other standard methods, we have kept the inbreeding coefficients for our fox population between 0.02 and 0.07. That means that whenever a fox pup with a novel trait has been born into the herd, the probability that it acquired the trait through inbreeding (that is, by

inheriting both of its mutant genes from the same ancestor) has varied between only 2 and 7 percent.

20 Second, some of the new traits are not recessive: They are controlled by dominant or incompletely dominant genes. Any fox with one of those genes would have shown its effects; there could have been no "hidden carriers" in the original population. Another, subtler possibility is that the novelties in our domesticated population are classic by-products of strong selection for a quantitative trait. In genetics, quantitative traits are characteristics that can vary over a range of possibilities; unlike Gregor Mendel's peas, which were either smooth or wrinkly with no middle ground, quantitative traits such as an animal's size, the amount of milk it produces or its overall friendliness toward human beings can be high, low or anywhere in between. What makes selecting for quantitative traits so perilous is that they (or at least the part of them that is genetic) tend to be controlled not by single genes but by complex systems of genes, known as polygenes. Because polygenes are so intricate, anything that tampers with them runs the risk of upsetting other parts of an organism's genetic machinery. In the case of our foxes, a breeding program that alters a polygene might upset the genetic balance in some animals, causing them to show unusual new traits, most of them harmful to the fox. Note that in this argument, it does not matter whether the trait being selected for is tameness or some other quantitative trait. Any breeding program that affects a polygene might have similar effects.

21 The problem with that explanation is that it does not explain why we see the particular mutations we do see. If disrupted polygenes are responsible, then the effects of a selection experiment ought to depend strongly on which mutations already existed in the population. If Belyaev had started with 130 foxes from, say, North America, then their descendants today would have ended up with a completely different set of novelties. Domesticating a population of wolves, or pigs, or cattle ought to produce novel traits more different still. Yet as Belyaev pointed out, when we look at the changes in other domesticated animals, the most striking things about them are not how diverse they are, but how similar. Different animals, domesticated by different people at different times in different parts of the world, appear to have passed through the same morphological and physiological evolutionary pathways. How can that be?

22 According to Belyaev, the answer is not that domestication selects for a quantitative trait but that it selects for a behavioral one. He considered genetic transformations of behavior to be the key factor entraining other genetic events. Many of the polygenes determining behavior may be regulatory, engaged in stabilizing an organism's early

development, or ontogenesis. Ontogenesis is an extremely delicate process. In principle, even slight shifts in the sequence of events could throw it into chaos. Thus the genes that orchestrate those events and keep them on track have a powerful role to play. Which genes are they? Although numerous genes interact to stabilize an organism's development, the lead role belongs to the genes that control the functioning of the neural and endocrine systems. Yet those same genes also govern the systems that control an animal's behavior, including its friendliness or hostility toward human beings. So, in principle, selecting animals for behavioral traits can fundamentally alter the development of an organism.

23 As our breeding program has progressed, we have indeed observed changes in some of the animals' neurochemical and neurohormonal mechanisms. For example, we have measured a steady drop in the hormone-producing activity of the foxes' adrenal glands. Among several other roles in the body, the adrenal cortex comes into play when an animal has to adapt to stress. It releases hormones such as corticosteroids, which stimulate the body to extract energy from its reserves of fats and proteins.

24 After 12 generations of selective breeding, the basal levels of corticosteroids in the blood plasma of our domesticated foxes had dropped to slightly more than half the level in a control group. After 28 to 30 generations of selection, the level had halved again. The adrenal cortex in our foxes also responds less sharply when the foxes are subjected to emotional stress. Selection has even affected the neurochemistry of our foxes' brains. Changes have taken place in the serotonin system, thought to be the leading mediator inhibiting animals' aggressive behavior. Compared with a control group, the brains of our domesticated foxes contain higher levels of serotonin; of its major metabolite, 5-oxyindolacetic acid; and of tryptophan hydroxylase, the key enzyme of serotonin synthesis. Serotonin, like other neurotransmitters, is critically involved in shaping an animal's development from its earliest stages: Selection and Development

25 Evidently, then, selecting foxes for domestication may have triggered profound changes in the mechanisms that regulate their development. In particular, most of the novel traits and other changes in the foxes seem to result from shifts in the rates of certain ontogenetic processes—in other words, from changes in timing. This fact is clear enough for some of the novelties mentioned above, such as the earlier eye opening and response to noises and the delayed onset of the fear response to unknown stimuli. But it also can explain some of the less obvious ones. Floppy ears, for example, are characteristic of newborn fox pups but may get carried over to adulthood.

26 Even novel coat colors may be attributable to changes in the timing of embryonic development. One of the earliest novel traits we observed in our domesticated foxes was a loss of pigment in parts of the head and body. Belyaev determined that this piebald pattern is governed by a gene that he named Star. Later my colleague Lyudmila Prasolova and I discovered that the Star gene affects the migration rate of melanoblasts, the embryonic precursors of the pigment cells (melanocytes) that give color to an animal's fur. Melanocytes form in the embryonic fox's neural crest and later move to various parts of the embryo's epidermis. Normally this migration starts around days 28 to 31 of the embryo's development. In foxes that carry even a single copy of the Star gene, however, melanoblasts pass into the potentially depigmented areas of the epidermis two days later, on average. That delay may lead to the death of the tardy melanoblasts, thus altering the pigmentation in ways that give rise to the distinctive Star pattern.

27 One developmental trend to which we have devoted particular attention has to do with the growth of the skull. In 1990 and 1991, after noticing abnormal developments in the skulls and jaws of some of our foxes, we decided to study variations in the animals' cranial traits. Of course, changes in the shape of the skull are among the most obvious ways in which dogs differ from wolves. As I mentioned earlier,

Morey believes that they are a result of selection (either natural or artificial) for reproductive timing and smaller body size.

28 In our breeding experiment, we have selected foxes only for behavior, not size; if anything, our foxes may be slightly longer, on average, than the ones Belyaev started with 40 years ago. Nevertheless, we found that their skulls have been changing. In our domesticated foxes of both sexes, cranial height and width tended to be smaller, and snouts tended to be shorter and wider, than those of a control group of farmed foxes. Another interesting change is that the cranial morphology of domesticated adult males became somewhat "feminized." In farmed foxes, the crania of males tended to be larger in volume than those of females, and various other proportions differed sharply between the sexes. In the domesticated foxes the sexual dimorphism decreased. The differences in volume remained, but in other respects the skulls of males became more like those of females. Analysis of cranial allometry showed that the changes in skull proportions result either from changes in the timing of the first appearance of particular structures or from changes in their growth rates. Because we studied the skulls only of adult foxes, however, we cannot judge whether any of these changes are pedomorphic, as Morey believes they are in dogs.

29 The most significant changes in developmental timing

in our foxes may be the smallest ones: those that have to do with reproduction. In the wild, foxes reach sexual maturity when they are about 8 months old. They are strict seasonal breeders, mating once a year in response to changes in the length of the day (in Siberia the mating season runs from late January to late March) and giving birth to litters ranging from one to 13 pups, with an average of four or five. Natural selection has hard-wired these traits into foxes with little or no genetic variation. Fur farmers have tried for decades to breed foxes that would reproduce more often than annually, but all their attempts have failed. In our experimental fox population, however, some reproductive traits have changed in a correlated manner. The domesticated foxes reach sexual maturity about a month earlier than nondomesticated foxes do, and they give birth to litters that are, on average, one pup larger. The mating season has lengthened. Some females breed out of season, in November–December or April–May, and a few of them have mated twice a year. Only a very small number of our vixens have shown such unusual behavior, and in 40 years, no offspring of an extraseasonal mating has survived to adulthood.

30 Nevertheless, the striking fact is that, to our knowledge, out-of-season mating has never been previously observed in foxes experiencing a natural photoperiod. Forty years into our unique lifelong experiment, we believe that Dmitry Belyaev would be pleased with its progress. By intense selective breeding, we have compressed into a few decades an ancient process that originally unfolded over thousands of years. Before our eyes, "the Beast" has turned into "Beauty," as the aggressive behavior of our herd's wild progenitors entirely disappeared. We have watched new morphological traits emerge, a process previously known only from archaeological evidence. Now we know that these changes can burst into a population early in domestication, triggered by the stresses of captivity, and that many of them result from changes in the timing of developmental processes. In some cases the changes in timing, such as earlier sexual maturity or retarded growth of somatic characters, resemble pedomorphosis. Some long-standing puzzles remain. We believed at the start that foxes could be made to reproduce twice a year and all year round, like dogs. We would like to understand why this has turned out not to be quite so. We are also curious about how the vocal repertoire of foxes changes under domestication. Some of the calls of our adult foxes resemble those of dogs and, like those of dogs, appear to be holdovers from puppyhood, but only further study will reveal the details.

31 The biggest unanswered question is just how much further our selective-breeding experiment

can go. The domestic fox is not a domestic dog, but we believe that it has the genetic potential to become more and more doglike. We can continue to increase that potential through further breeding, but the foxes will realize it fully only through close contact with human beings. Over the years, other investigators and I have raised several fox pups in domestic conditions, either in the laboratory or at home as pets. They have shown themselves to be good-tempered creatures, as devoted as dogs but as independent as cats, capable of forming deep-rooted pair bonds with human beings—mutual bonds, as those of us who work with them know. If our experiment should continue, and if fox pups could be raised and trained the way dog puppies are now, there is no telling what sort of animal they might one day become.

32 Whether that will happen remains to be seen. For the first time in 40 years, the future of our domestication experiment is in doubt, jeopardized by the continuing crisis of the Russian economy. In 1996 the population of our breeding herd stood at 700. In 1998, with no funds to feed the foxes or to pay the salaries of our staff, we had to cut the number to 100. Earlier we were able to cover most of our expenses by selling the pelts of the foxes culled from the breeding herd. Now that source of revenue has all but dried up, leaving us increasingly dependent on outside funding at a time when shrinking budgets and changes in the grant-awarding system in Russia are making long-term experiments such as ours harder and harder to sustain. Like many other enterprises in our country, we are becoming more entrepreneurial. Recently we have sold some of our foxes to Scandinavian fur breeders, who have been pressured by animal-rights groups to develop animals that do not suffer stress in captivity. We also plan to market pups as house pets, a commercial venture that should lead to some interesting, if informal, experiments in its own right. Many avenues of both applied and basic research remain for us to pursue, provided we save our unique fox population.

Post-Reading

Basic Comprehension

MULTIPLE CHOICE

Circle the choice that best answers each question.

1. Why does Trut believe that "[i]n many ways, though, the question of intentionality is beside the point" (Paragraph 1)?

    a. Her research group is not interested in the morphological and behavioral changes in dogs.

    b. It may be impossible and unnecessary to separate natural from artificial selection.

    c. Once wolves and humans started to live together, only artificial selection and not natural selection took place.

    d. Scientists have long ignored the question of intentionality.

2. Which trait was NOT identified by Morey as a result of natural selection operating on some dogs?

    a. The bone structure of their heads was different from that of other dogs.

    b. Their bodies did not become as large as adult wolves.

    c. They became sexually mature at a later age than did wolves.

    d. They continued to whine, bark, and be submissive as they grew older.

3. According to Paragraph 5, Belyaev's approach to genetics was

    a. similar to Trofim Lysenko's

    b. different in 1959 from what it was in 1948

    c. more closely related to animal physiology

    d. in agreement with Darwinian ideas

4. According to Belyaev's theory, selecting for tame behavioral responses results in similar changes across widely different mammal species. This happens because

    a. in all different species, tameness is related to the control of certain chemicals

    b. all the different species have the same hormones and neurotransmitters

    c. widely different animals are from the same taxonomic groups

    d. many different species share the same set of regulatory genes

5. What can be most strongly inferred from Paragraph 9 about defensive behavior in animals?

   a. It is more strongly affected by an embryo's pre-birth environment than by genes.
   b. It is stronger and more obvious in domestic individuals than in wild individuals.
   c. Trut and her colleagues believed it weakened as tamability increased.
   d. Trut and her colleagues believed a strong form of it helped animals reproduce successfully.

6. Which is the most likely reason why the researchers did not train the foxes used in the domestication study? (see Paragraph 11)

   a. The foxes, which came from fox farms, had already been trained.
   b. The researchers did not have enough time to train as many foxes as were used in the study.
   c. Mother foxes might reject any pups that had been trained by humans.
   d. Training by itself can result in greater tameness regardless of inherent tamability.

7. In Paragraph 14, Trut mentions foxes that ran away from the farm. What does she most strongly imply about these foxes?

   a. That they were treated cruelly during the experiment
   b. That they had originally come from the wild and wanted to return
   c. That they lacked the abilities necessary to feed and protect themselves in the wild
   d. That they were sick or injured when they came back to the farm

8. What reasons does Trut give to explain why changes in the fox population were probably not caused by inbreeding? (Paragraphs 18–20) (Choose two.)

   a. Some of the new traits would have been observed in the founding population if these traits had come from there.
   b. The fox population was so large that genetically related foxes almost never mated with each other.
   c. The new traits observed among Trut's foxes differed from those of foxes domesticated at different places and times.
   d. The researchers mated experimental foxes with non-experimental foxes from time to time.

9. According to the reading's description of neurochemical and neurohormonal mechanisms in the experimental foxes in Paragraphs 23 and 24, which of the following is true?

a. The behavior of domesticated foxes is not greatly influenced by neurohormones or neurotransmitters.

b. Domesticated foxes are fatter and less energetic than wild foxes.

c. Populations selected for domestic behaviors develop chemical characteristics different from those of unselected populations.

d. Selecting for chemical characteristics is scientifically more reliable than selecting for behaviors.

10. According to Trut's explanation, what do loss of pigment in parts of the body, earlier eye opening, and floppy ears in domesticated foxes have in common?

a. They are unique to foxes among domesticated species.

b. They involve the migration of melanoblasts.

c. They result from selecting for certain physical traits.

d. They can be explained by changes in developmental timing.

SHORT ANSWER

Answer the questions in your own words.

1. According to the introduction, what aspect of canine domestication do evolutionary theorists have questions about?

_____

_____

_____

2a. According to Trut's and Belyaev's theory of domestication, what selective factor causes the changes observed in domesticated species?

_____

_____

_____

2b. How does selecting for this factor lead to physical, behavioral, and morphological changes?

_____

_____

_____

2c. According to this theory, why are the changes to different domesticated species similar in nature?

_____

_____

_____

3. How is Belyaev's theory of domestication similar to and different from Morey's theory?

_____

_____

_____

4. Cross out all of the following that are NOT pieces of evidence Trut uses to support her theory and explain how she uses the evidence to support her theory.

   a. behavioral signs of domestication such as friendliness and eagerness to be around humans
   b. changes to the physical bodies of domesticated foxes
   c. similarities between traits developed by unrelated groups of foxes subjected to the same conditions
   d. changes to the biochemical mechanisms of the domesticated foxes
   e. trainability of the domesticated foxes

5. Why was the future of the fox domestication experiment in jeopardy at the time the article was written?

_____

_____

_____

TEXTUAL EVIDENCE

Part 1. Put an X next to each of the questions that Trut's article answers.

_____ Can silver foxes be domesticated?

_____ Were dogs domesticated deliberately?

_____ How many generations does it take to domesticate silver foxes?

_____ Do domesticated foxes demonstrate similar traits to domesticated dogs?

_____ Does selection for pedomorphic traits explain most of the tameness in domesticated horses, cats, etc.?

_____ Can a wide range of changes to domesticated species result from selection for a behavioral trait?

_____ Might domesticated foxes make good pets?

Part 2. Which of the questions marked with an X in Part 1 do you think Belyaev was most interested in answering? Rank them with the one being most interesting to Belyaev at the top of your ranking. Discuss your ranking with a partner or in a small group.

Vocabulary

NEAR SYNONYMS

Read the paraphrases of some of the points Trut makes in the reading. Cross out the word or phrase in parentheses that is most different in meaning from the others. Then write a new sentence using the crossed-out word appropriately.

1. Theorists wonder whether the domestication of dogs was (drastic, deliberate, intentional, planned).

   _____

   _____

   _____

2. We are left to (bear out, consider, ponder, speculate about) what additional changes might occur to silver foxes if they continue to be bred for tamability.

   _____

   _____

   _____

3. Part of the purpose of the experiment was to determine whether observed differences between domesticated animals and their wild ancestors (are attributable to, are triggered by, interact with, stem from) selection for a behavioral trait.

   _____

   _____

   _____

4. The domesticated foxes (display, exhibit, mirror, show) friendliness toward humans.

   _____

   _____

   _____

MULTIPLE CHOICE

Choose the word or phrase closest in meaning to the italicized words in each sentence from the reading.

1. "To test his hypothesis, Belyaev decided to turn back the clock to the point at which animals received the first *challenge of domestication.*"

   a. pressure to become domesticated
   b. difficulty caused by being domesticated
   c. experiments to domesticate them
   d. physical changes due to domestication

2. "In 1948, his commitment to *orthodox* genetics had cost him his job as head of the Department of Fur Animal Breeding at the Central Research Laboratory of Fur Breeding in Moscow."

   a. conventional
   b. cutting-edge
   c. mammalian
   d. scientific

3. "Now, 40 years and 45,000 foxes after Belyaev began, our experiment has achieved *an array* of concrete results."

   a. a final conclusion
   b. a great reward
   c. a interesting finding
   d. a wide range

4. "Another, subtler possibility is that the novelties in our domesticated population are classic *by-products* of strong selection for a quantitative trait."

   a. research reports
   b. direct causes
   c. population characteristics
   d. extra results

5. "In some cases the changes in timing, such as earlier sexual maturity or *retarded* growth of somatic characters, resemble pedomorphosis."

   a. decreased
   b. delayed
   c. earlier
   d. increased

6. "Before our eyes, 'the Beast' has turned into 'Beauty,' as the aggressive behavior of our *herd's* wild progenitors entirely disappeared."

   a. group's
   b. experiment's
   c. country's
   d. audience's

PARAPHRASING

According to the article, "When scientists ponder how animals came to be domesticated, they almost inevitably wind up thinking about dogs." If something is *inevitable*, it always happens or is unavoidable. *Inevitably* is the adverb form. Paraphrase the sentences to use the word *inevitable* or *inevitably*.

1. It seems domestication of animals always involves physiological and morphological changes as well as behavioral changes.

    _____

    _____

2. Every fox that escaped the farm came back. _____

    _____

    _____

3. If the scientists don't receive more funding, they will be forced to shut down their experiment. _____

    _____

    _____

According to the article, "Belyaev believed that similarity in the patterns of these traits was the result of selection for amenability to domestication." If something is *amenable to* something, it is readily acted on by that thing. *Amenable to* should be followed by a noun phrase, not by a verb. *Amenability* is the noun form. Paraphrase the sentences to use the word *amenable* or *amenability*.

4. Some species seem incapable of being domesticated because they are not suited to domestication. _____

    _____

    _____

5. One behavioral difference between the domestic species *Canis familiaris* and *Felis domesticus* is that dogs submit to human orders more readily than cats. _____

    _____

    _____

6. Faced with funding cuts, some of the researchers reacted favorably to the suggestion that the lab make money by selling foxes as pets.

    _____

    _____

Reading Focus
Putting Reading to Work

COMPLETION

Lyudmila Trut's article describes a number of morphological, physiological, and behavioral differences between her experiments on the domesticated foxes and other foxes. In Column A, write a sentence describing the difference in each category listed. All the information can be found in the reading. In Column B, write an explanation of how the changes might support Morey's and/or Belyaev's theories. This information can also be found in the reading, but it may be stated indirectly or implied. In Column C, write at least one question that still remains and keeps Belyaev's theory from being confirmed. These questions may not be directly or indirectly stated in the reading but will come from deep understanding and analysis of the text. The first set has been done for you as an example.

A. Differences between domesticated foxes and farmed or wild foxes	B. How these differences support Morey's and/or Belyaev's theories	C. Questions that are not answered by these findings
Behavior: *The domesticated foxes are tame and seek to please humans and to receive human attention.*	*This behavior includes whining, submissiveness, and pedomorphic traits, which could support Morey's theory. It is also behavior that is influenced by changes to developmental mechanisms, which could support Belyaev's theory.*	*Would similar behavior emerge if species taxonomically more different from dogs were selected for tamability?*
Development in early life:		

A. Differences between domesticated foxes and farmed or wild foxes	B. How these differences support Morey's and/or Belyaev's theories	C. Questions that are not answered by these findings
Appearance:		
Biochemical mechanisms:		
Reproduction:		

DISCUSSION

Share your questions from Column C with a partner or in a small group. Decide the top five outstanding questions that remain to be answered before Belyaev's theory can be confirmed. Then design an experiment that would answer as many of these questions as possible.

FOLLOW UP

In her conclusion, published in 1999, Trut stated that the future of the silver fox domestication experiments were in jeopardy. Do some research and answer one of the questions. Your answer could be given in writing or as a presentation in class.

1. What happened to the foxes used in the study or their descendents? How does this relate to points made in Trut's article?

2. Have Trut and her colleagues continued their domestication research? How do recent findings relate to the findings published in the article?

3. How has research by other researchers confirmed, expanded on, or refuted Trut's findings?

Integrating Information

The readings in this unit have discussed ways in which species can be altered so they possess traits useful to humans. Trut's article focused on a process for domesticating a wild species, while Pollan's piece focused on issues surrounding genetic engineering of an already domesticated species and increased corporate control over agriculture.

Companies are looking for new ways to produce food while reducing the toll human food production takes on the environment. Some are attempting to domesticate wild species prized by humans as food, such as the bluefin tuna. Others are adding genes to make crops like rice more nutritious or more hardy.

WRITING

Do some research about one such attempt to genetically modify food. Use one or two reference sources to write a paragraph explaining how issues raised in this unit are related to that attempt. You may use print or online sources.

UNIT 2

Surviving Extremes

Adventurers do not need to go beyond Earth to find environments that threaten human life. This unit describes the body's responses to threatening circumstances on this planet. The unit is organized as follows:

- FIRST TIER: Human Survival
  Book review: **Life on the Edge** by Mike Stroud

- SECOND TIER: Human Heat Tolerance
  Journal article: **Extremes of Human Heat Tolerance: Life at the Precipice of Thermoregulatory Failure** by W. Larry Kenney, David W. DeGroot, and Lacy Alexander Holowatz

- THIRD TIER: Hypothermia
  Government pamphlet: **Hypothermia—The Cold Facts** by Timothy W. Smalley

First Tier: Human Survival

Pre-Reading

DISCUSSION

This reading is a book review. The author gives his opinion about a book written by someone else. Based on the title of the review, "Life on the Edge," and that of the book being reviewed, *The Biology of Human Survival: Life and Death in Extreme Environments,* answer the questions and make predictions about what you will read. Discuss them with other students.

1. Do you think the reader will need to know a lot about science in order to understand the book?
2. What types of science will be mentioned in the book?
3. What is an extreme environment?
4. Can you think of any places that have extreme environments? Where are they?

Reading

Life on the Edge

Mike Stroud

BOOK REVIEWED—**The Biology of Human Survival:**
Life and Death in Extreme Environments
by Claude A. Piantadosi
Oxford University Press: 2003. 280 pp.

1 Stories of human achievements and survival against the odds have always been fascinating. Whether in the context of simply living in the world's harshest environments, mounting expeditions to its hottest, coldest, highest or deepest places, or coping with the aftermath of disaster, everybody wonders at just how the body copes. Answers lie in the study of environmental physiology, the responses and adaptations that can take men and women to extremes.

2 *The Biology of Human Survival* is an extraordinary environmental physiology text. The topics covered range far beyond biology to include the physics and function of artificial aids that allow humans to cope with extremely hostile environments. But engineering approaches are not just used to describe life-supporting technologies—the

author also uses them to explain biological concepts. This approach helped me to understand some concepts that I had previously struggled with. Occasionally, however, the opposite applies.

3 The book begins by describing the limits to the range of environments that can support human life, along with the principles of survival, adaptation and life-support systems. The historical background to environmental physiology is fascinating, but as the book moves on to adaptation (physiological changes in response to environmental stress) and maladaption (adverse changes resulting from adaptation), some topics were unclear and others were made unnecessarily complex. For example, the author stresses the importance of discriminating between technical definitions, such as adaptation, acclimatization, acclimation, accommodation and habituation, but then, I feel, blurs the boundaries. He has also focused particularly on maladaption and cross-acclimation (adaptive changes to one type of environmental stress that prove beneficial during exposure to stress from a different type of environment), perhaps ascribing more importance to these processes than they deserve. Indeed, he suggests that adverse effects of cross-acclimation between cold and hypoxic responses contribute to the difficulty of climbing Mount Everest

in winter. In reality, this must be insignificant compared to winter's cold, storms and jet-stream winds.

4 But back to the book's strengths. Several chapters cover adaptation to heat and cold in detail. There are lengthy descriptions of human responses and adaptation to icy environments, but our physiological responses to heat (which are far more effective than those to cold) are not covered in such depth. This book is not, then, a definitive work on environmental physiology. But viewed as a collection of thought-provoking pieces about this field it becomes a tour de force. This is especially true when the author strays from his title, covering not just engineering and biology, but also life that is far from human. The piece on the physiology of the camel in the section on salt and water is masterly, and there are fascinating descriptions of the interaction between primitive life and Earth's early atmosphere. There is also a beautifully worked analysis of why you should never drink sea water.

5 The chapter on nutrition and survival, although generally excellent, does perpetuate some rather outdated views. For example, it states that the main difference between the forms of malnutrition known as marasmus and kwashiorkor is in the level of protein intake; elsewhere in the book, the author mentions the more current idea

that kwashiorkor and its accompanying oedema are more a product of free-radical membrane damage than low protein ingestion. There is also misleading information about the subsequent reintroduction of normal nutrition (refeeding), and there are some rather simplistic views on vitamin deficiency. These include the idea that the main problem with vitamin A depletion is ocular, whereas we now know that vitamin A deficiency also impairs responses to infections of the gut and respiratory tract, leading to deaths in people who have very little or no eye damage.

6 Biology and engineering are mixed even more freely in the second half of the book than in the first. Descriptions of the technical engineering solutions to the high pressures of the deep sea and low pressures of the high mountains are balanced excellently with descriptions of pressure physiology and the illnesses that can stem from pressure change. Just as in the earlier part of the book, in which problems caused by the cold are illustrated by compelling tales including those of Scott of the Antarctic and the *Titanic*, the author uses famous disasters to bring the issues in this section to life. The sinking of the Russian submarine *Kursk* is used to great effect.

7 Towards the end of the book there is a surprising but topical diversion into survival in the face of nuclear, biological and chemical weapons of mass destruction. This is a rather depressing digression, but it is both interesting and relevant.

8 The book ends with a section lifting us away from Earth's limitations to describe the exciting physiology and engineering of high-performance aircraft and space flight. The final chapter even speculates on the requirements for and limitations to future human colonization of other planets, and so ends on a positive note, as will I. There is no doubt that this book will be enjoyed widely and will be much appreciated by both specialists and scientifically thoughtful lay readers.

Mike Stroud is at the Institute of Human Nutrition, Tremona Road, Southampton SO16 6YD, UK. His expeditions to the Earth's extremes include ultra-distance runs in the Sahara and the first unsupported walk across Antarctica.

Post-Reading

Basic Comprehension

SHORT ANSWER

Answer the questions in your own words.

1. After reading the article, review your pre-reading predictions for Questions 1 and 2 on page 53. Which of your predictions were right? Which were not?

   _____

   _____

   _____

2. Which extreme environments are mentioned in the book review? How many did you list in your answers to Questions 3 and 4 on page 53?

   _____

   _____

   _____

3. What aspect of Piantadosi's book did the reviewer like most? What did he like least?

   _____

   _____

   _____

MATCHING

Match the words in the left column with the best description from the right column. Each letter should be used only once.

___ 1. adaptation

___ 2. cross-acclimation

___ 3. engineering

___ 4. maladaptation

___ 5. malnutrition

___ 6. physiology

a. not getting enough good food

b. making designs for machines, buildings, and artificial systems

c. how your body is structured and how it works

d. changes to suit one environment that help you do better in another

e. changes that make it harder to live in a harsh environment

f. changes that help you do better in a harsh environment

MULTIPLE CHOICE

Circle the choice that best answers each question.

1. Which of the statements is closest to the main idea of the reading?
   a. Despite certain weaknesses, readers interested in science will enjoy Piantadosi's book.
   b. Despite the outdated facts in the book, readers will enjoy its humorous tales.
   c. The book is too technical for most audiences, but it's a good reference for specialists.
   d. The book will be appreciated by engineers, but probably not by biologists.

2. According to the description in the reading, what is the main topic of *The Biology of Human Survival*?
   a. illnesses and injuries with environmental causes
   b. engineering approaches to survival in harsh environments
   c. biological adaptation to extreme environments
   d. the importance of discriminating among technical definitions

3. Which is closest in meaning to "Occasionally, however, the opposite applies." in Paragraph 2?

   a. Piantadosi's biological approach to engineering sometimes makes the technological concepts easier to understand.

   b. Piantadosi's biological approach to engineering sometimes makes the technological concepts more difficult to understand.

   c. Piantadosi's engineering approach to biology sometimes makes the biological concepts easier to understand.

   d. Piantadosi's engineering approach to biology sometimes makes the biological concepts more difficult to understand.

4. Which criticism is NOT made by the reviewer?

   a. Piantadosi does not deal with the complexity of adaptation and maladaptation.

   b. Piantadosi draws an unlikely conclusion regarding the difficulty of climbing Mount Everest.

   c. Piantadosi exaggerates the importance of maladaptation and cross-acclimation.

   d. Piantadosi is not always precise in his use of technical terms.

5. According to the reading, which statement best represents a modern understanding of nutrition?

   a. The primary difference between kwashiorkor and marasmus is the level of protein ingestion.

   b. Kwashiorkor has more to do with free-radical damage than protein intake.

   c. The main damage from vitamin A deficiency occurs in the eyes.

   d. Vitamin A deficiency leads to problems in the gut and respiratory tract but does not kill.

DRAWING CONCLUSIONS

Based on the information provided in the reading, which questions would you expect to see answered in Piantadosi's book? Check (✓) those you consider most likely to be answered. Discuss your answers with other students.

1. What is the coldest environment in which humans can survive? ____

2. How do human adaptations to cold and hypoxic conditions affect mountain climbing? ____

3. What is the difference between acclimatization and acclimation? ____

4. What is the current understanding of human physiological heat responses? ____

5. How do camels survive for long periods without taking in water? ____

6. What happens to humans if they drink sea water? ____

7. What combination of vitamins and minerals is ideal for maintaining good health? ____

8. What problems occur to the human body due to high or low pressures? ____

9. How does technology help people survive in high or low pressures? ____

10. How can we prevent terrorist attacks that use weapons of mass destruction? ____

11. How might humans survive on other planets? ____

Vocabulary

SHORT ANSWER

Answer the questions about the vocabulary used in the reading.

1. The reading dealt with a book about environmental physiology. Using a dictionary, find out what precisely the word *physiology* means. How does the meaning of this word overlap with and differ from each of the following terms?

   biology _____

   body _____

   anatomy _____

   form _____

2. Rank the environments from 1 (**least hostile**) to 7 (**most hostile**) to human survival. Provide a brief reason for your choice for each ranking.

   a. ___ outer space _____

   b. ___ the Sahara Desert _____

   c. ___ Antarctica _____

   d. ___ tropical rainforests _____

   e. ___ temperate grasslands _____

   f. ___ the desert southwestern United States _____

   g. ___ the arctic north coast of North America _____

MATCHING

Match each phrase on the left with the phrase on the right that most closely relates to it.

1. a way the body *copes with* high temperatures (Paragraphs 1 and 2) _____

2. the *aftermath* of a flood (Paragraph 1) _____

3. *ascribing* too much importance to a single cause (Paragraph 3) _____

4. a *definitive* dictionary (Paragraph 4) _____

5. something that might cause one's mind to *stray from* one's studies (Paragraph 4) _____

6. *perpetuating* a falsehood (Paragraph 5) _____

7. a *compelling* tale (Paragraph 6) _____

8. a *diversion* in a book about human physiology (Paragraph 7) _____

9. *lay readers* (Paragraph 8) _____

a. a fascinating or interesting story

b. the sound of an interesting TV show coming from another room

c. sweating

d. causing people to continue to believe a lie

e. people without specialized knowledge on the topic

f. the loss of life and property as a result of or subsequent to it

g. not paying enough attention to other reasons for something

h. a digression or departure from the topic

i. a book that contains all of the words in a language, leaving out none

Reading Focus

Grouping Information

CAUSES AND EFFECTS

Find effects mentioned in the book review. List the effects in the left column. In the right column, write causes from the list. Some causes will be used more than once. Also, some effects have more than one cause. One item is done for you as an example.

cross-acclimation between cold
    and hypoxic reactions
differences in level of protein
    intake
extreme cold
free-radical membrane damage

infections of the gut and
    respiratory tract
jet-stream winds
pressure change
storms
Vitamin A deficiency

Effects	Causes
eye damage	*Vitamin A deficiency*

CATEGORIZING

Arrange the aspects of *The Biology of Human Survival* according to whether the reviewer thinks Piantadosi's treatment of them is strong or weak. The reviewer comments both positively and negatively about them.

chapters on adaptation to heat and cold

coverage of all aspects of environmental physiology

discussion of survival in the face of weapons of mass destruction

explanation of adaptation and maladaptation in general

explanation of the history of environmental physiology

final-chapter explanation of how malnourished people are re-fed

speculation about how humans might survive on other planets

the overall impression the book gave

use of engineering to explain biological concepts

use of engineering to explain life-supporting technologies

use of stories about famous disasters

Treated Strongly	Treated Weakly

Integrating Information

WRITING

Do some research to write a paragraph on one of the questions.

1. Have you heard the compelling tales of problems caused by cold and pressure mentioned in the reading (the Scott expedition in Antarctica, the sinking of the *Titanic*, and the sinking of the *Kursk*)? What do you know about these events that make them relevant to the book?

2. Have you heard or read any amazing stories of human survival in extreme conditions? What conditions did the people face? What physical effects did the danger have on them? How did they survive?

Second Tier: Human Heat Tolerance

Pre-Reading

DISCUSSION

Articles in academic journals often include an abstract, or brief summary, of the article at the beginning. Read the abstract on page 67 and answer the questions.

1. In your own words, what main topics do you think this reading will cover?

2. Why do you think many academic journals include a list of keywords?

MATCHING

The abstract ends with a list of key words. They will be important in the reading. Guess what they mean. Write the letter of the best definition or description. After you finish the reading, come back and check your guesses.

____ 1. heat stroke

____ 2. hyperthermia

____ 3. prescriptive zone

____ 4. sweating

____ 5. thermal balance

____ 6. thermoregulation

a. a body temperature much higher than normal

b. producing moisture through the skin

c. controlling the temperature of something

d. maintaining a steady core temperature in the body

e. damage to the body caused by excessively high temperatures

f. a range of temperatures normal for the human body

Note: The reading contains technical shorthand—short symbols like T_c that stand for concepts.

- Each symbol is defined the first time it is used.
- As you read, you can understand these by thinking of the words they stand for. For example, when you see T_c think "body core temperature."
- You do not have to remember the symbols. Focus on the ideas, not on the shorthand.

Reading

Extremes of Human Heat Tolerance: Life at the Precipice of Thermoregulatory Failure

W. Larry Kenney, David W. DeGroot and
Lacy Alexander Holowatz

Abstract

1 Human life is sustainable only below an internal temperature of roughly 42–44°C. Yet our ability to survive at severe environmental extremes is testimony to the marvels of integrative human physiology.

2 One approach to understanding human thermoregulatory capacity is to examine the upper limits of thermal balance between man and the air environment, i.e. the maximal environmental conditions under which humans can maintain a steady-state core temperature. Heat acclimation expands the zone of thermal balance.

3 Human beings can and do, often willingly, tolerate extreme heat stresses well above these thermal balance limits. Survival in all such cases is limited to abbreviated exposure times, which in turn are limited by the robustness of the thermoregulatory response.

4 Figures are provided that relate tolerance time and the rate of change in core temperature to environmental characteristics based on data compiled from the literature.

Keywords: Thermoregulation; Thermal balance; Sweating; Prescriptive zone; Hyperthermia; Heat stroke

Article Outline

1. Introduction

1 The topic of "environmental extremes" for humans seems relatively straightforward on the surface, yet researching such a topic proves more difficult. "Extreme" thermal environments have different connotations to different people, even the thermal physiologists who conduct research on the topic of human thermoregulation. Certainly there are extremes at either end of the environmental temperature spectrum, and cold tolerance is equally important to heat tolerance from a teleological perspective. For brevity sake, the present paper deals only with extremes of heat. One may characterize a thermal extreme as the upper limit of humans' ability to maintain thermal balance, as defined by a steady state core temperature. This approach has been used in laboratory studies and a discussion of the topic begins the present treatise.

2 While defining the upper limit of thermal balance is instructive, human beings can and do tolerate extreme heat stresses well above these equilibration limits, albeit for short periods of time. A popularly retold story goes as follows:

> One morning toward the end of the eighteenth century, the Secretary of the Royal Society of London, one Mr. Blagden, ventured into a room heated to 105°C, taking with him some eggs, a piece of raw steak and a dog. A quarter of an hour later, the eggs were baked hard and the steak cooked to a crisp but Blagden and his dog walked out unharmed . . . (Ashcroft, 2000)

3 Mr. Blagden's experiment vividly points out how tolerant humans truly are to dry heat—provided that free evaporation of sweat can occur, hot surface temperatures are avoided (Blagden's dog was kept in a basket to keep it from burning its feet), the circulatory system can compensate, and the exposure time is limited.

4 While the above story is astonishing, situations in which human beings tolerate such extremes form the basis for the second part of this paper. The highest recorded temperature on earth is apparently 58°C in the Sahara and many deserts routinely reach 45°C (Ashcroft, 2000). Sauna temperatures typically range from 80 to 100°C with relative humidity (rh) as low as 5%, and bathers commonly spend 15–30 min or more in these extreme temperatures. The primary physiological compensatory mechanism during these exposures is evaporative heat loss from sustainable sweating. This results in progressive dehydration and cardiovascular strain, especially in the absence of fluid and electrolyte replacement. Where the preceding conditions rely on evaporative heat loss, other environments rely almost exclusively on integrated cardiovascular responses to compensate for the heat load (such as hot water immersion). The hottest Japanese *onsen* (spa baths)

are 46–47°C, yet experienced bathers routinely tolerate these temperatures for ~3 min. In summary, humans can tolerate considerable extremes of thermal stress, relying on different compensatory mechanisms depending on the characteristics of the environment.

2. Limits to Human Heat Balance

5 Over a wide range of environments, body core temperature (T_c) equilibrates at temperatures proportional to metabolic rate, independent of ambient conditions (Saltin and Hermansen, 1966). Thermal environments above this designated "prescriptive zone" (Lind, 1963) do not allow thermal balance either because of excessive dry heat gain or limited evaporative heat loss, and the result is a continuous rise in T_c. Conditions which define the upper limit of the prescriptive zone or "psychrometric limit" for a given metabolic heat production represent one type of environmental "extreme" and such balance points have been determined experimentally for heat-acclimated men (Belding and Kamon, 1973) and women (Kamon and Avellini, 1976), as well as for unacclimated men and women (Kenney and Zeman, 2002).

6 Experiments are conducted in a programmable environmental chamber. The experimental protocol involves the determination of either (1) the critical water vapor pressure (P_{crit}) for the upward inflection of T_c at several distinct dry-bulb temperatures (T_{db}), or (2) the critical dry-bulb temperature (T_{crit}) at several distinct ambient water vapor pressures (P_a). The methods used to determine P_{crit} and T_{crit} have been previously described in detail (Belding and Kamon, 1973; Kamon and Avellini, 1976; Kenney, 1988). During the T_{crit} experiments, P_a is held constant and T_{db} is systematically increased approximately 1°C every 5 min after a 30-min equilibration period. In the P_{crit} experiments, T_{db} is held constant while P_a is increased approximately 1 Torr every 5 min after a similar equilibration period. During each test, the subjects walked continuously on a motor-driven treadmill for up to 3 h at a pre-determined exercise intensity. Air velocity (v) was also varied in some experiments. Typically, T_c begins to plateau by about 40 min and remains at an elevated steady state as P_a or T_{db} is increased. The critical environment is defined as that immediately before the upward T_c inflection, i.e. the combination of conditions below which thermal balance can be maintained, but above which a steady rise in T_c occurs.

7 Fig. 1 presents a portion of a psychrometric chart showing data compiled from two sets of experiments performed in our laboratory some 25 years apart (Kamon and Avellini, 1976; Kenney and Zeman, 2002). Each point shown is the mean from several subjects and each line represents the extreme critical environments below which T_c can achieve a biophysi-

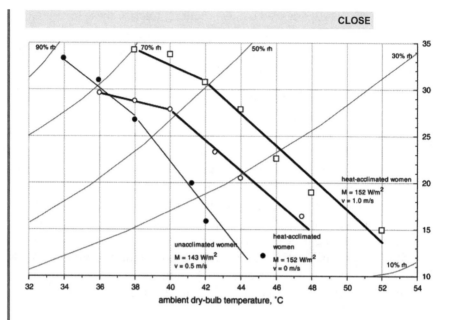

Fig. 1. Psychrometric representation of upper limits of thermal balance determined from Penn State experiments. Each line represents such an upper limit, analogous to Lind's "upper limit of the prescriptive zone." The filled circles and lighter line are from unacclimated subjects (Kenney and Zeman, 2002), while the open circles and squares are for heat-acclimated women (Kamon and Avellini, 1976). Heat acclimation shifts the lines upward and to the right, increasing the range of environments in which heat balance is possible for a given metabolic rate *(M)* and air velocity *(v)*. Similarly, increasing v shifts the curve further to the right. Each data point represents the mean results from a cohort of subjects.

cal steady state, but above which T_c rises continuously. The effect of heat acclimation is to shift the line rightward, encompassing more environmental conditions below the psychrometric limit. Increased velocity of air movement around the subject is another factor that shifts the psychrometric limit rightward and upward.

3. Environmental Extremes

3.1. Dry Heat

8 Extreme dry heat presents a severe challenge to homeostasis. Yet human beings have demonstrated a remarkable capacity to withstand, and adapt to, the extreme physiological stresses desert conditions demand. To dissipate heat gained in a desert environment, the free evaporation of sweat is coupled with an elevation in skin blood flow. Tolerance time in dry heat depends on the sustainable sweating rate and the ability to withstand the resultant dehydration. The following is an anecdotal account of extended desert exposure.

9 In 1994, Mauro Prosperi became lost in a sandstorm during the 160-mile Marathon des Sables in the Moroccan desert (Kamler, 2004). On day 4 of the event, scheduled as a 50-mile leg of the race in an ambient temperature of 46°C (115°F), Prosperi lost his way in a sandstorm and wandered off course. With less that one full canteen of water, he survived for 9 days. During his ordeal, he drank his own urine and sought shelter in an empty Muslim shrine, where he ate bats he was able to catch in the shrine. He restricted his movement to the cooler parts of the day and night. The following is a description of Prosperi after he was rescued and brought to an Algerian hospital:

> . . . doctors reported that the desert wanderer had lost 33 pounds and that 16 liters of intravenous fluids were needed to replace his water loss. His kidneys were barely functioning, his liver was damaged, and he was unable to digest food. His eyes had sunk back inside their sockets, and his skin was dry and wrinkled. He looked like a tortoise. But he would survive.

10 Assuming that this amazing tale is true, it may be the most extreme documented case of survivable dehydration.

11 *Physiology of dry heat exposure*: The ability to withstand extreme heat exposure depends on the aerobic fitness, hydration status, and heat acclimation status of the subject. In the ensuing discussions of the physiological adaptations that make it possible for subjects to tolerate exposure to extreme temperatures, such assumptions are necessary for tolerance to, and survival in, true extremes of environment.

12 The primary physiological compensatory mechanism during exposure to dry heat is evaporative cooling. Unofficially, the highest sweating rate recorded is 5.6 L/h (liters per hour), a rate based on the >3 kg body weight loss of a professional tennis player in a laboratory setting over a 50-min period of exercise (Dr. Robert Murray, Ph.D., personal communication). Exercise consisted of cycling at 75–95 percent of maximum heart rate and voluntary fluid consumption was 1.6 L. The environmental chamber was 35°C and 63% relative humidity (rh), with minimal air movement. In the published literature the highest reported sweating rate may be that of Olympic distance runner Alberto Salazar. Based on body weight change during the 1984 Olympic Marathon, and compensating for *estimated* fluid consumption, Salazar had a reported sweating rate of 3.7 L/h. During testing in an environmental chamber earlier that year, his measured sweating rate was 2.8 L/h (Armstrong et al., 1986).

13 Hypohydration caused by high sweating rates in the absence of adequate fluid replacement leads to elevations in T_c, relative to a euhydrated state, and an increased rate of heat storage, thereby decreasing tolerance

time. Hypohydration leads to cardiovascular strain by reducing cardiac filling pressure, reducing stroke volume and causing a compensatory increase in heart rate (Sawka and Pandolf, 1990). Sawka (Sawka et al., 1985) investigated the influence of heat stress and graded hypohydration (0, 3, 5, 7% body weight) during exercise at 49°C, 20% rh. Higher levels of hypohydration resulted in a greater incidence of exhaustion (exercise termination) at a given T_c, such that a 7% reduction in body weight decreased time to exhaustion from 140 min (at 0 and 3% dehydration) to 64 min. Additionally, hypohydration led to a predictable increase in heart rate and T_c for each exercise bout. Interestingly, two of the subjects terminated the exercise due to the appearance of premature ventricular contractions, suggesting that this level of ~7% hypohydration may be near the tolerable safe limit. We are unaware of experimentally induced hypohydration exceeding 8% of body weight.

3.2. Non-Evaporative Environments

14 A distinctly different hot environment in comparison to the desert is one in which both ambient heat and ambient water vapor pressure are high. The robustness of the cardiovascular response and the ability to tolerate profound elevations in T_c determine tolerance time in this situation. The most extreme example of a non-evaporative environment is hot water immersion. In this environment most avenues of heat loss are unavailable, as skin temperature quickly equilibrates with water temperature and evaporative cooling is limited to any skin surface not immersed in water. Immersed skin cannot dissipate heat through evaporation, and radiation and conduction become avenues of heat gain. One extreme example of hot water immersion is the Japanese *onsen*, ancient stone communal baths where the hottest water temperatures are reported to be 46–47°C. Most bathers can only withstand these extreme temperatures for 3 min (Ashcroft, 2000). However, Japanese people customarily bathe in 40°C water for periods of up to 60 min. The following is an account of a Westerner's first experience with the Japanese *onsen*.

> I stepped boldly into the pool—and leapt straight out again. It was scalding hot. At least 45°C. I thought I must have first-degree burns. . . . When I emerged from my pool five minutes later I was a bright cherry red, like a boiled lobster. All of my blood had been directed to my skin as my body tried desperately to cool down—to no avail, for not only could I not get rid of the heat I generated myself, but I was rapidly accumulating that of the bath. I sat on the edge of the pool, my skin pouring sweat. But I felt marvellous . . . for although a short dip is marvellously invigorating, to remain there too long would, quite literally, be fatal.

15 Warm water SCUBA diving is a unique example of thermoregulatory stress that adds metabolic heat production in addition to hot water immersion. Rescue divers working in warm water wear vulcanized rubber suits and carry equipment that can weigh up to 45 kg. These divers can experience increases in T_c as high as 3°C during a 1-h rescue mission (White et al., 1998). Rescue operations are carried out with dive pair teams with one diver remaining on the surface, where evaporative cooling is still limited by the wet suit. White (White et al., 1998) measured T_c changes during both warm and cold water rescue training sessions; the ambient temperature for the warm water training rescue situation was 23°C and the water temperature was 21°C. These investigators found that the mean increase in T_c in all divers was 1.2°C, however 2 divers had an increase in T_c greater than 2°C in 30–50 min. T_c continued to climb even after exiting the water at the conclusion of the training session. This situation represents another example of extreme heat stress because evaporative cooling is severely limited while metabolic heat is being generated causing core temperature to climb rapidly.

16 *Physiological responses to extreme non-evaporative heat*: In the laboratory, a standard method to test subjects' upper limits of thermal tolerance is the water-perfused suit. In numerous experiments (Minson et al., 1998; Rowell et al., 1970; Rowell, 1974, Rowell, 1983 and Rowell, 1986) investigators raised skin temperature to 40°C by the use of these tube-filled suits to examine the cardiovascular adjustments to severe hyperthermia. This experimental paradigm maximizes skin blood flow and allows for investigation of integrated cardiovascular adjustments when the $T_c–T_{sk}$[1] thermal gradient is reversed (as occurs in hot water immersion as well).

17 When subjects are heated to thermal tolerance using water-perfused suits, an integrated cardiovascular response ensues. During severe hyperthermia, skin blood flow can increase to as much as 7–8 L/min. To support this increase in skin blood flow, cardiac output is raised by 3 L/min/°C rise in right atrial blood temperature (Rowell, 1986). This increase is primarily mediated through an increase in heart rate although small increases in stroke volume do occur, despite the falling right atrial filling pressure. Additionally, approximately 0.6 L/min of blood is redistributed to the skin from the splanchnic circulation, and 0.4 L/min of blood from the renal circulation. Muscle blood flow may also be reduced during passive heat stress and redirected toward the cutaneous circulation. Due to the volume of blood in the cutaneous circulation and the lack of muscle pump activity, right atrial pressure declines.

---

[1] T_{sk} = skin temperature

3.3. Heat Tolerance: Duration of Exposure

18 While anecdotal accounts of extreme heat exposure provide some qualitative insight into the limits of human heat tolerance, laboratory experiments over the decades have provided ample data relating tolerance time to a given set of environmental characteristics. Numerous investigators have measured the "maximal" tolerance time in a given environment, and have used that information to determine "safe" exposure limits. Fig. 2 and Fig. 3 are drawn using data compiled from the literature in an attempt to examine the nature of the relation between environment, rate of rise in T_c, and tolerance time. To be included in this analysis, experiments had to satisfy several critical criteria. These studies needed to report the time to exhaustion for the group, the change in T_c (or provide enough data to calculate this variable), and a description of the subject's activity level. Addi-

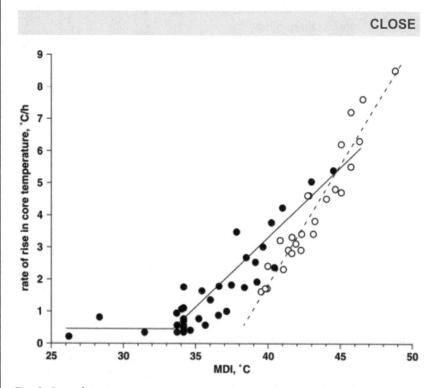

CLOSE

Fig. 2. Rate of rise in core temperature plotted against the mean discomfort index (MDI, a measure of the combined non-radiant thermal environment similar to WBGT). These data points were derived from a series of published studies meeting finite criteria. Open circles are from resting exposures while filled circles come from exercise trials. Above an MDI of about 32°C, both responses are linear (resting: $y = 7.4x-2.8$, $R^2 = 0.92$; exercise: $y = 4.3x-1.4$, $R^2 = 0.84$).

tionally, chamber T_{db}[2] and either T_{wb}[3] or rh were necessary. As few laboratory studies over the years have included globe temperature data (a measure of radiant heat load), calculation of wet-bulb globe temperature (WBGT) across the studies was not possible. Alternatively, the modified discomfort index (MDI) proposed by Moran and Pandolf (1999) was calculated. Briefly, the MDI is calculated as $(0.75T_{wb}) + (0.30T_{db})$ and correlates well with WBGT ($r > 0.95$). Fig. 2 presents data for the rate of change in T_c/h as a function of MDI, compiled from several studies meeting the aforementioned criteria (Avellini et al., 1980; Goldman et al., 1965; Iampietro and Goldman, 1965; Nag et al., 1999 and Nag et al., 1997; Pandolf et al., 1988; Randle and Legg, 1985; Sawka et al., 1983 and Sawka et al., 1992; Shapiro et al., 1980; Shvartz and Benor, 1972). Compared to resting

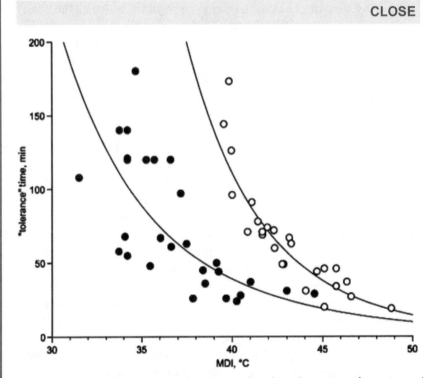

Fig. 3. "Tolerance" time (time to exhaustion or physiological cessation of experimental session) plotted against the modified discomfort index (MDI). These data points were derived from a series of published studies meeting finite criteria. Open circles are from resting exposures while filled circles come from exercise trials. Each relationship is well represented by an exponential function, with the exercise relationship shifted to the left relative to resting data.

---

[2] T_{db} = temperature as measured by a dry—bulb thermometer.

[3] T_{wb} = temperature as measured by a wet—bulb thermometer.

exposure, exercise is associated with a larger rate of change in T_c/h in a given environment, in part because of the additional cardiovascular strain superimposed on the thermoregulatory strain. The highest absolute change in T_c recorded was 2.6°C (several studies only reported the per hour value, and the absolute T_c change was not reported). Fig. 3 shows the relationship between tolerance time (time to exhaustion or test termination) and MDI. During either resting or exercising conditions, an increase in MDI reduced tolerance time in a relatively predictable fashion. However, exercise data are again shifted to the left.

4. *Thermoregulatory Failure*

19 Heat stroke is traditionally defined as a rectal temperature greater than 40.6°C, with untoward neurological involvement. This condition is the consequence of severe cardiovascular strain accompanied by thermoregulatory failure. In heat stroke, the internal heat load overwhelms the capacity of the system, and the maintenance of core temperature is sacrificed so that arterial pressure and blood flow to vital organs may be better maintained (Rowell, 1986). The ensuing cardiovascular strain due to heat and progressive dehydration causes a reduction in skin blood flow and sweating and a rapid increase in core temperature. Heat stroke is often associated with multiple organ system damage including cognitive impairment, acute renal failure, rhabdomyolysis, liver dysfunction with hepatic enzyme elevation, disseminated intravascular coagulation, and acid base disturbances (Sutton, 1990).

20 While a T_c in excess of 42°C is usually considered fatal, T_c correlates poorly with the severity of organ dysfunction (Gardner and Kark, 2001). The highest T_c survived without lasting complications was 46.5°C (Slovis et al., 1982). On that day, the ambient high T_{db} was 38°C, with 44% rh. The 52-year-old male victim reported that he had been cooking indoors all day in a poorly ventilated room. Emergency medical services were summoned when the victim failed to answer his door. Medical personnel recorded a rectal temperature at the scene of 42°C, which represented the upper limit of their thermometer. Upon arriving at the hospital, and 25 min after aggressive cooling had been initiated, doctors recorded a rectal temperature of 46.5°C. Calibration of the thermometer was validated later that day. In spite of the severe hyperthermia, liver and renal complications, and disseminated intravascular coagulation, the patient survived and was discharged after 24 days of hospitalization.

5. *Summary*

21 This paper has attempted to present anecdotes, clinical cases, and results of laboratory experiments related to extremes of heat stress. The

purpose has been twofold: to examine environmental "extremes" in their many facets, and to highlight the exquisite precision and adaptability of human thermoregulation.

References

Armstrong et al., 1986 L.E. Armstrong, R. Hubbard, B. Jones and J. Daniels, Preparing Alberto Salazar for the heat of the 1984 Olympic Marathon, *Physician and Sportsmedicine* 14 (1986), pp. 73–81.

Ashcroft, 2000 F. Ashcroft, Life at the Extremes The Science of Survival, University of California Press, Berkeley (2000).

Avellini et al., 1980 B.A. Avellini, Y. Shapiro, K.B. Pandolf, N.A. Pimental and R.F. Goldman, Physiological responses of men and women to prolonged dry heat exposure, *Aviation, Space, Environ. Med.* 51 (1980), pp. 1081–1085.

Belding and Kamon, 1973 H.S. Belding and E. Kamon, Evaporative coefficients for prediction of safe limits in prolonged exposures to work under hot conditions, *Federation Proc.* 32 (1973), pp. 1598–1601.

Gardner and Kark, 2001 J. Gardner and J. Kark, Clinical diagnosis, management, and surveillance of exertional heat illness In: K.B. Pandolf and R. Burr, Editors, *Medical Aspects of Harsh Environments*, Office of the Surgeon General, US Army, Falls Church, VA (2001), pp. 231–279.

Goldman et al., 1965 R. Goldman, E. Green and P.F. Iampietro, Tolerance of hot, wet environments by resting men, *J. Appl. Physiol.* 20 (1965), pp. 271–277.

Iampietro and Goldman, 1965 P.F. Iampietro and R.F. Goldman, Tolerance of man working in hot, humid environments, *J. Appl. Physiol.* 20 (1965), pp. 73–76.

Kamler, 2004 K. Kamler, Surviving the Extremes A Doctor's Journal to the Limits of Human Endurance, St. Martin's Press, New York, NY (2004).

Kamon and Avellini, 1976 E. Kamon and B. Avellini, Physiologic limits to work in the heat and evaporative coefficient for women, *J. Appl. Physiol.* 41 (1976), pp. 71–76.

Kenney, 1988 W.L. Kenney, Control of heat-induced cutaneous vasodilation in relation to age, *Eur. J. Appl. Physiol.* 57 (1988), pp. 120–125.

Kenney and Zeman, 2002 W.L. Kenney and M.J. Zeman, Psychrometric limits and critical evaporative coefficients for unacclimated men and women, *J. Appl. Physiol.* 92 (2002), pp. 2256–2263.

Lind, 1963 A.R. Lind, A physiological criterion for setting thermal environmental limits for everyday work, *J. Appl. Physiol.* 18 (1963), pp. 51–56.

Minson et al., 1998 C.T. Minson, S.L. Wladkowski, A.F. Cardell, J.A. Pawel-czyk and W.L. Kenney, Age alters the cardiovascular response to direct passive heating, J. Appl. Physiol. 84 (1998), pp. 1323–1332.

Moran and Pandolf, 1999 D.S. Moran and K.B. Pandolf, Wet bulb globe temperature (WBGT)—to what extent is GT essential?, Aviat. Space Environ. Med. 70 (1999), pp. 480–484.

Nag et al., 1997 P.K. Nag, S.P. Ashtekar, A. Nag, D. Kothari, P. Bandyopad-hyay and H. Desai, Human heat tolerance in simulated environment, Indian J. Med. Res. 105 (1997), pp. 226–234.

Nag et al., 1999 A. Nag, D. Kothari and H. Desai, Exposure limits of women in hot environment, Indian J. Med. Res. 110 (1999), pp. 138–144.

Pandolf, 1988 K.B. Pandolf, B. Cadarette, M.N. Sawka, A.J. Young, R. Fransesconi and R.R. Gonzalez, Thermoregulatory responses of middle-aged and young men during dry-heat acclimation, J. Appl. Physiol. 65 (1988), pp. 65–71.

Randle and Legg, 1985 I.P. Randle and S.J. Legg, A comparison of the effects of mixed static and dynamic work with mainly dynamic work in hot conditions, Eur. J. Appl. Physiol. Occup. Physiol. 54 (1985), pp. 201–206.

Rowell, 1974 L.B. Rowell, Human cardiovascular adjustments to exercise and thermal stress, Physiol. Rev. 54 (1974), pp. 75–159.

Rowell, 1983 L.B. Rowell, Cardiovascular aspects of human thermoregulation, Circ. Res. 52 (1983), pp. 367–379.

Rowell, 1986 L.B. Rowell, Human Circulation Regulation During Physical Stress, Oxford University Press, New York (1986).

Rowell et al., 1970 L.B. Rowell, G.L. Brengelmann, J.R. Blackmon and J.A. Murray, Redistribution of blood flow during sustained high skin temperature in resting man, J. Appl. Physiol. 28(1970), pp. 415–420.

Saltin and Hermansen, 1966 B. Saltin and L. Hermansen, Esophageal, rectal, and muscle temperature during exercise, J. Appl. Physiol. 21 (1966), pp. 1757–1762.

Sawka and Pandolf, 1990 M.N. Sawka and K.B. Pandolf, Effects of body water loss on physiological function and exercise performance In: C. Gisolfi and D. Lamb, Editors, Fluid Homeostasis During Exercise, Cooper Publishing Group, Traverse City, MI (1990), pp. 1–38.

Sawka et al., 1983 M.N. Sawka, M.M. Toner, R.P. Francesconi and K.B. Pandolf, Hypohydration and exercise effects of heat acclimation, gender, and environment, J. Appl. Physiol. 55 (1983), pp. 1147–1153.

Sawka et al., 1985 M.N. Sawka, A.J. Young, R.P. Francesconi, S.R. Muza and K.B. Pandolf, Thermoregulatory and blood responses during exercise at graded hypohydration levels, J. Appl. Physiol. 59 (1985), pp. 1394–1401.

Sawka et al., 1992 M.N. Sawka, A.J. Young, W.A. Latzka, P.D. Neufer, M.D. Quigley and K.B. Pandolf, Human tolerance to heat strain during exercise influence of hydration, J. *Appl. Physiol.* 73 (1992), pp. 368–375.

Shapiro et al., 1980 Y. Shapiro, K.B. Pandolf, B.A. Avellini, N.A. Pimental and R.F. Goldman, Physiological responses of men and women to humid and dry heat, J. *Appl. Physiol.* 49 (1980), pp. 1–8.

Shvartz and Benor, 1972 E. Shvartz and D. Benor, Heat strain in hot and humid environments, *Aerospace Med.* 43 (1972), pp. 852–855.

Slovis et al., 1982 C.M. Slovis, G.F. Anderson and A. Casolaro, Survival in a heat stroke victim with a core temperature in excess of 46.5 C, *Ann. Emerg. Med.* 11 (1982), pp. 269–271.

Sutton, 1990 J. Sutton, Clinical Implications of Fluid Imbalance In: C. Gisolfi and D. Lamb, Editors, *Fluid Homeostasis During Exercise*, Cooper Publishing Group, Traverse City, MI (1990), pp. 425–448.

White et al., 1998 L.J. White, F. Jackson, M.J. McMullen, J. Lystad, J.S. Jones and R.H. Hubers, Continuous core temperature monitoring of search and rescue divers during extreme conditions, *Prehospital Emerg. Care* 2 (1998), pp. 280–284.

Post-Reading

Basic Comprehension

MULTIPLE CHOICE

Circle the choice that best answers each question.

1. In Paragraph 2 the author writes, "While defining the upper limit of thermal balance is instructive, human beings can and do tolerate extreme heat stresses well above these equilibration limits, albeit for short periods of time." Which statement best paraphrases the main point of this sentence?

   a. Defining the maximum heat stress under which a thermal balance can be maintained is instructive.

   b. For short times, humans can survive high temperatures under which they cannot maintain a thermal balance.

   c. Humans can maintain thermal equilibrium above the upper limit of thermal balance only for short times.

   d. The upper limit of thermal balance varies depending on both heat stress and time period.

2. Which is NOT mentioned as a reason Mr. Blagden and his dog survived a room heated to 105°C?

   a. They didn't stay in contact with hot surfaces.
   b. They drank plenty of water.
   c. They lost heat by sweating.
   d. They stayed in the room for a short time.

3. Humans commonly tolerate sauna temperatures from 80–100°C for 15–30 minutes, while they tolerate the hottest Japanese *onsen* at the lower temperature of 46–47°C for only up to three minutes. All of the following statements EXCEPT one help explain this. According to the reading, which one does NOT?

   a. In *onsen*, the body's cardiovascular response helps determine how long a person can remain immersed.
   b. In saunas, humans can lose heat through radiation and evaporation.
   c. In the air of dry saunas, the body gains heat through processes like conduction.
   d. In the water of *onsen*, blood rushes to the skin surface.

4. In referring to Figure 1, Paragraph 7 says, "Increased velocity of air movement around the subject is another factor that shifts the psychometric limit upward and rightward." Which statement best expresses the essential information in that sentence?

   a. Subjects in the experiment felt dangerously warm earlier when fast-moving air was directed toward them.
   b. Subjects felt dangerously warm later when fast-moving air was directed toward them.
   c. Subjects never felt dangerously warm later when fast-moving air was directed toward them.
   d. Subjects felt the same in fast-moving air as when no moving air was directed toward them.

5. In Paragraph 11, the author mentions "aerobic fitness, hydration status, and heat acclimation status" because

   a. each factor is tested separately in one of the experiments mentioned later
   b. researchers have no way to measure any of these factors
   c. these factors are psychometric, not physiological, so they do not influence experimental results
   d. these factors influence tolerance of great heat in every experiment described here

6. According to the information in Paragraph 13, what is the heart's response to sweating a lot without replacing fluids?

   a. It attempts to lower blood pressure.
   b. It beats faster.
   c. It beats slower.
   d. It compensates for high blood pressure.

7. Why is the ability to tolerate profound elevations in core temperature more important in situations of high ambient heat and high ambient water vapor pressure than in hot desert environments?

   a. Less evaporative compensation is possible.
   b. Less radiation and conduction occur.
   c. No cardiovascular response occurs.
   d. Skin temperature remains cooler than core temperature.

8. What does Paragraph 15 imply about the core temperatures of divers in two-person warm-water rescue teams?

   a. The core temperatures of both divers increase.
   b. The core temperature of the diver on the surface rises while that of the other diver falls.
   c. The core temperatures of both divers decrease.
   d. The core temperature of the diver on the surface falls while that of the other diver rises.

9. Which statement is true about the human cardiovascular response to heat, according to the reading?

   a. Stroke volume rises in response to both dry and wet heat extremes.
   b. Heart rate rises in response to both dry and wet heat extremes.
   c. Stroke volume rises in response to dry heat extremes but drops in response to wet heat extremes.
   d. Heart rate rises in response to dry heat extremes but drops in response to wet heat extremes.

10. Why does the word *maximal* appear in quotation marks in Paragraph 18?

    a. To indicate maximal times were not actually reached, only estimated.
    b. To indicate that it is used as a specific technical term by investigators.
    c. To emphasize how extreme these conditions were
    d. To emphasize that the experiments were not conducted scientifically and their results are questionable.

11. In Paragraph 18, what does it mean in Figure 3 that "exercise data are again shifted to the left"?

    a. Tolerance time during exercise increased as subjects became accustomed to increased MDI levels.
    b. Tolerance time during rest periods increased as subjects became accustomed to increased MDI levels.
    c. Tolerance time was greater at a given MDI level during exercise conditions than during resting conditions.
    d. Tolerance time was lower at a given MDI level during exercise conditions than during resting conditions.

12. Which condition is NOT mentioned in the reading as being associated with heat stroke?

    a. Blood flow to the skin decreases.
    b. Core temperature cannot be maintained.
    c. The sweating rate rises rapidly.
    d. The heart strains to maintain blood pressure for major organs.

BEST EXPLANATION

The Westerner experiencing a Japanese *onsen* for the first time stated, "All of my blood had been directed to my skin as my body tried desperately to cool down—to no avail, for not only could I not get rid of the heat I generated myself, but I was rapidly accumulating that of the bath." Circle the number of the sentence in Paragraph 14 that best expresses the principle behind this observation.

① A distinctly different hot environment in comparison to the desert is one in which both ambient heat and ambient water vapor pressure are high. ② The robustness of the cardiovascular response and the ability to tolerate profound elevations in T_c determine tolerance time in this situation. ③ The most extreme example of a non-evaporative environment is hot water immersion. ④ In this environment most avenues of heat loss are unavailable, as skin temperature quickly equilibrates with water temperature and evaporative cooling is limited to any skin surface not immersed in water. ⑤ Immersed skin cannot dissipate heat through evaporation, and radiation and conduction become avenues of heat gain. ⑥ One extreme example of hot water immersion is the Japanese *onsen*, ancient stone communal baths where the hottest water temperatures are reported to be 46–47°C. ⑦ Most bathers can only withstand these extreme temperatures for ~3 min (Ashcroft, 2000). ⑧ However, Japanese people customarily bathe in 40°C water for periods of up to 60 min. ⑨ The following is an account of a Westerner's first experience with the Japanese *onsen*.

Vocabulary

MULTIPLE CHOICE

Choose the word or phrase closest in meaning to each italicized word or phrase in the sentences from the reading.

1. "Human beings can and do, often willingly, *tolerate* extreme heat stresses well above these thermal balance limits."

   a. adapt to
   b. recognize
   c. suffer from
   d. withstand

2. "Mr. Blagden's experiment vividly points out how tolerant humans truly are to dry heat—provided that free evaporation of sweat can occur, hot surface temperatures are avoided (Blagden's dog was kept in a basket to keep it from burning its feet), the circulatory system can *compensate*, and the exposure time is limited."

   a. go into operation
   b. make adjustments
   c. shut down
   d. heat up

3. "Conditions which define the upper limit of the prescriptive zone or 'psychrometric limit' for a given metabolic heat production represent one type of environmental 'extreme' and such balance points have been determined experimentally for heat-*acclimated* men."

   a. exposed
   b. liking
   c. productive
   d. adapted

4. "Figure 1 presents a portion of a psychometric chart showing data *compiled* from two sets of experiments performed in our laboratory some 25 years apart."

   a. put together
   b. discovered
   c. estimated
   d. calculated

5. "This results in *progressive* dehydration and cardiovascular strain, especially in the absence of fluid and electrolyte replacement."

   a. fatal
   b. excessive
   c. increasing
   d. positive

6. "Air *velocity* (*v*) was also varied in some experiments."

   a. composition
   b. humidity
   c. speed
   d. temperature

7. "Immersed skin cannot *dissipate* heat through evaporation, and radiation and conduction become avenues of heat gain."

   a. avoid
   b. deal with
   c. distribute
   d. get rid of

8. "In this environment most avenues of heat loss are unavailable, as skin temperature quickly equilibrates with water temperature and evaporative cooling is limited to any skin surface not *immersed in water.*"

   a. covered by
   b. exposed to
   c. heated by
   d. moistened by

9. "In heat stroke, the internal heat load overwhelms *the capacity of the system*, and the maintenance of core temperature is sacrificed so that arterial pressure and blood flow to vital organs may be better maintained."

   a. body parts at the extremities of the system
   b. how much the system can handle
   c. the average
   d. the temperature of the system as a whole

10. "In heat stroke, the internal heat load *overwhelms* the capacity of the system, and the maintenance of core temperature is sacrificed so that arterial pressure and blood flow to vital organs may be better maintained."

    a. catches up with

    b. is too great for

    c. is in balance with

    d. causes an increase in

ANTONYM MATCHING

Match the italicized word in each sentence from the reading with the word or phrase in the box that is most nearly the opposite in meaning.

begin	give way to	mild
external	impossible to maintain	reduction
fatiguing	insufficient	weakness

1. Human life is only *sustainable* within a certain range of temperatures. _____

2. *Excessive* heat can lead to heat stroke. _____

3. Humans can *withstand* water temperatures of 46–47°C only for a few minutes. _____

4. An *elevation* of blood flow to the skin helps release heat in dry environments. _____

5. The subjects had to *terminate* the experiment when they felt too much discomfort. _____

6. Excessive heat provides a *severe* challenge to the body. _____

7. Some people find a dip in a very hot bath to be *invigorating*. _____

8. In heat stroke, a person's *internal* temperature rises sharply. _____

9. The *robustness* of the cardiovascular response is a key factor in how well humans can tolerate heat in water. _____

PARAPHRASING

Rewrite the sentences in the matching exercise to express a related idea using the antonyms.

1. _____
   _____

2. _____
   _____

3. _____
   _____

4. _____
   _____

5. _____
   _____

6. _____
   _____

7. _____
   _____

8. _____
   _____

9. _____
   _____

Reading Focus

SCANNING FOR NUMBERS

Scan the reading for the temperatures. Next to each temperature, list its significance to human survival. In extreme survival cases, list the amount of time humans did or can survive.

1. 105°C _____

2. 80–100°C _____

3. 58°C _____

4. 46–47°C _____

5. 46.5°C _____

6. 45°C _____

7. 42°C _____

8. 40.6°C _____

9. 40°C _____

Word Parts

The first reading of this unit contains the words *maladaptation* and the more common word *malnutrition*. Someone suffering from malnutrition does not get enough healthy food—has poor nutrition. *Mal-* means "bad." *Maladaptation* involves adapting in ways poorly suited to an environment. Technical writing often contains words like this created by combining word parts derived from Latin or Greek.

MATCHING

Match each word part on the left with its meaning on the right. Base your answers on your knowledge of word parts and on the context of the reading.

1. therm _____   a. good; well

2. meter _____   b. heat

3. hyper _____   c. heart

4. hydr _____   d. less than normal

5. de _____   e. more than normal

6. hypo _____   f. related to blood vessels

7. eu _____   g. remove

8. intra _____   h. something that measures

9. vascular _____   i. water

10. cardi _____   j. within

WRITING DEFINITIONS

Using your knowledge of word parts, write a definition of each word.

  1. cardiac _____

  2. cardiovascular _____

  3. dehydration _____

  4. euhydrated _____

  5. hydration _____

  6. hyperthermic _____

  7. hypohydration _____

  8. intravascular _____

  9. thermal _____

10. thermometer _____

11. thermoregulatory _____

Describing Processes

EXPRESSING RELATIONSHIPS

Write a sentence to express a relationship between the two concepts in each pair. Use a connecting word or phrase from the box in each of your sentences. Use each connecting word or phrase only once.

ensue   lead to   result from   result in   the consequence of

excessive sweating and dehydration

sweating in dry air and evaporative heat loss

organ damage and heat stroke

divers remaining at the surface being unable to benefit from evaporative cooling and their rubber suits

cardiovascular response and heating to thermal tolerance

Putting Reading to Work

WRITING

Do some research on ONE of these questions. Use one or two reference sources outside this chapter to gather information. You may use print or online sources. Write a short report (about 250 words) comparing the information you find in your research to the information in the reading.

1. This article discussed human reactions to extreme temperatures in detail. Choose another species of organism that survives in extremely hot environments. How is this species' adaptations to heat similar to and different from human adaptations?

2. This article discussed cardiovascular responses to extremely high temperatures. How does this compare to how the human cardiovascular system reacts to extremely low temperatures?

Third Tier : Hypothermia

Pre-Reading

DISCUSSION

In Tier 2 you read about differences in the human body's ability to deal with heat in wet and dry environments. Tier 3 deals with hypothermia. Before you read, discuss the questions in a small group.

1. Based on Tier 2 and on your own knowledge, what differences would you expect between the body's ability to deal with cold air and with cold water?

2. In what circumstances would people experience hypothermia, or low body temperature?

3. In those circumstances, what should a person do to avoid hypothermia? If someone gets hypothermia, what should be done to avoid serious harm?

4. If you encounter a hypothermia victim, what should you do to try to help?

Reading

Hypothermia—The Cold Facts

Cold Water Facts . . .

- Hypothermia means losing heat faster than your body can produce it.
- For most of the year, water in Minnesota lakes is cold enough to kill you.
- Alcohol doesn't make you warmer, but it does impair balance, coordination and judgment.
- Hypothermia kills by eliminating your ability to swim and stay afloat.
- Hypothermia symptoms include continual shivering, numbness, poor coordination, slurred speech and personality changes.
- A strong swimmer has only about a 50/50 chance of reaching shore one-half mile away in 50° water.
- Most hypothermia deaths involve non-PFD wearing victims who had no intention of entering the water.

Note: The reading often mentions temperatures (e.g. "50° water" or "mid-60s). These are on the Fahrenheit scale—as is normal in the United States. To convert to the Celsius scale, use this formula:

Temp F - 32(5/9) = Temp C

1 **Sunny skies and mid-60s temperatures** had kept the weather forecaster's promise of a pleasant September day in northern Minnesota, perfect for one last fishing trip before a Twin Cities couple put their 14-foot fishing boat away for the season. Beverly and Harold had spent the day fishing and were preparing to pull up anchor when disaster struck. Harold stood up and stumbled over a tackle box, causing the boat to capsize. Beverly was able to scramble to the top of the overturned craft, but each time her companion attempted to do the same, the boat started to roll, nearly pitching her into the lake. As a result, Harold remained immersed up to his neck in the 50-degree water. For most of the night, he clung to the side of the boat. About 2 A.M., Beverly felt the boat lurch and saw Harold's hat floating away on the moonlit water.

2 Although the accident report officially listed the cause of death as drowning, chances are the victim succumbed to an insidious killer that is involved in as many as perhaps 50 percent of all boating deaths: hypothermia.

The Big Chill

3 **Put simply,** hypothermia means that you are losing heat faster than your body can produce it, causing a drop in your inner (core) temperature. *Hypo* from Greek means below. *Thermic* refers to temperature. (Someone who is *hyper*-thermic has an *above* normal temperature, such as a fever.) Everyone has at one time or another experienced hypothermia. If you awoke this morning before your alarm clock sounded, chances are you were slightly hypothermic. Why? Your inner fire (known as the metabolism) had burned down because of a lack of fuel (food). You became cold and woke up. This slight lowering of temperature of one-half a degree is not really important. Only when your temperature drops to 95° or so does the situation become really serious.

4 Hypothermia can occur both in the water (acute hypothermia) or on land (chronic hypothermia). News stories often feature reports of lost hunters spending a night in the woods. When rescuers find them, the victims are described as suffering from "exposure." Exposure, an obsolete term for hypothermia,

describes the cause rather than the effect of the condition. In some cases, hypothermia can take hours or even days to creep up on victims. On the other hand, cold-water-immersion hypothermia usually happens very quickly. How quickly can depend on a number of factors. Among them are: age, weight, sex, physical and mental condition of the victim, water temperature, amount and type of clothing being worn, whether or not the victim is wearing a personal flotation device (PFD), and if the victim remains motionless, thrashes about, or tries to swim. Hypothermia usually kills immersed victims by eliminating their ability to swim or stay afloat. If the water is cold enough, even someone wearing a PFD will eventually die of cardiac arrest if he or she isn't rescued and rewarmed.

Cold Is Where You Find It

5 **Cold water is difficult to define,** even for experts. Generally water less than 70° is considered cold. At any temperature below 70°, most lightly clothed individuals will lose heat faster than they can produce it. Most bodies of water in Minnesota are below 70° for much of the year and certainly for the fall, winter, and spring. Half of all boating deaths occur in "off-season" months. **Alcohol and water, especially cold water, don't mix.**

A Quick Trip from Margaritaville to Hypothermiaville

6 **Many outdoor enthusiasts** insist upon taking a "little nip" now and then, thinking that drinking will help ward off the cold. Contrary to that popular notion, alcoholic beverages will not warm the body. Most hospitalized hypothermia cases involve people who have consumed excessive quantities of alcohol. The initial warm flush felt after drinking intoxicating beverages is caused by the expansion of the peripheral blood vessels (called vasodilation). This results in an increased blood flow to the skin, producing the familiar "glow" felt after a person takes the first drink. Alcohol induced vasodilation within the brain decreases the amount of oxygen reaching the brain cells. This explains the bizarre physical and psychological changes often brought about by intoxication. These changes impair short-term and long-term memory and inhibit an individual's ability to act in an appropriate manner to help themselves in an emergency situation. Shivering, a result of the rapid expansion and contraction of the skeletal muscles, is on the body's first line of defense against hypothermia. It warms the skin and provides a warning to find heat. (Approximately 10 percent of the

population does not shiver at all.) Increased quantities of warm blood, coursing through alcohol dilated blood vessels, fools the "heat sensors" located within the skin into relaying an "all's well" to the brain. This short circuits the mechanism that would normally trigger shivering—denying the body its most effective heat producing response.

Shock and Panic: Only the Strong (and the Smart) Survive

7 **If you unexpectedly plunge** into cold water, the first hazards you face are shock and panic. The physical shock of cold water upon the system causes increases in blood pressure, heart rate, and adrenaline levels. Cardiac arrest and death in a matter of minutes could follow. Cold water immersion shock also causes cold-induced gasping. Anyone who has ever stepped into a cold shower knows the effects of the "Torso Reflex." This is your automatic gasp for air in response to being hit in the chest area with cold water. If your mouth is underwater when this gasp occurs, drowning is the most probable outcome. If you know you are about to fall into cold water, cover your face with your hands. This helps you to avoid gasping water into your lungs. Panic has also been shown to be a significant factor in many drownings. A surprise dip in icy water can cause

panic in the most stalwart individuals. In an emergency situation, the lack of calm, clear thinking often results in drowning. In cold water you may experience violent shivering and intense pain. Just remember that these are natural body responses that are not life-threatening. You should take quick action before you lose full use of your hands: button up clothing, attempt to reboard, etc.

8 Studies have shown that "mental toughness" and a positive attitude about your survival and rescue will extend your survival time. Your WILL to LIVE does make a difference!

The Signpost up Ahead . . . The Hypothermia Zone

9 **Since cooling rates** for various individuals vary for the reasons discussed earlier, no two hypothermia victims will display exactly the same symptoms at exactly the same time. You must not rely on the victim's protests that they "feel fine." Why? Because hypothermia can cause confusion and abnormal behavior. Therefore, you must be acquainted with some of the signs of hypothermia to be able to render aid immediately.

Hypothermia Symptoms

10 Dr. Robert Pozos, a leading hypothermia researcher and former director of the Hypothermia and Water Safety Laboratory at the University of Minnesota—Duluth,

School of Medicine, recommends keeping a lookout for the following symptoms:

- *Continual shivering*
- *Poor coordination*
- *Slowing of pace—hanging back*
- *Increasingly numb hands and feet (this leads to stumbling, clumsiness, and loss of dexterity)*
- *Dazed and confused behavior (victim may be careless and forgetful)*
- *Slurred and slow speech (victim may be slow to respond to questions)*
- *Hallucinations*
- *Dilated pupils (open)*
- *Decreased attention span*
- *Changes in personality often to the exact opposite of victim's usual personality*

Dr. Pozos advises that if any of these symptoms appear, begin rewarming procedures immediately. If the victim recovers from these early symptoms in time, their chances of beating hypothermia are quite good. The longer you delay, the poorer his or her chances become.

Treatment

11 **Even the experts disagree** on the best treatment for the victims of hypothermia. What *is* agreed upon, however, is this: With a problem as serious as hypothermia, professional medical care should be sought as soon as possible—even for victims that have seemingly made a complete recovery. Complications such as neurologic, blood chemistry, and heart/lung disorders take their share of victims, sometimes after it appears they have recovered. Only a physician is qualified to pass medical judgment as to the condition of a hypothermia or near-drowning victim.

First Aid in the Field

12 **As soon as hypothermia victims** are taken from the water, they should be *gently* moved to a sheltered area. Wet clothes should be carefully cut off to avoid rough treatment and jostling that can cause physical shocks to internal organs. Dress the victim in layers of clothing or blankets. A knit-wool stocking cap will help reduce further heat loss from the head. Wrapping a scarf *loosely* around the neck and face will allow air to be pre-warmed before entering the victim's lungs and help retain body warmth. After taking these first steps to prevent further heat loss, seek medical assistance, but only if doing so does not endanger other members of your group.

13 Once medical assistance has been summoned, Dr. Pozos recommends these steps to rewarm the victim. If the victim is conscious:

- *Encourage movement (if shivering is not yet pronounced) unless the size of the shelter prevents it. Shelter is more important than movement at this point.*
- *Slowly feed the victim hot, sugary tea, hot chocolate, or bouillon*

(about 110°—slightly warm to the touch).

- Wrap the victim in a sleeping bag or several blankets.
- Try to keep the victim awake and talking.
- Keep the victim's head at least level with the body (some slight elevation of the legs and feet is desirable).
- In an open situation, move as many people as possible into the shelter so their body heat can warm the victim's immediate environment. Warm rocks or a fire (at a distance) will also help raise "local" temperature.

Active Rewarming

14 **These external rewarming techniques** can be easily employed in the field if you are sure that more aggressive procedures are necessary.

- Body-to-body contact. The victim and one or two "warmers" should be only lightly clothed rather than fully clothed. Two or more sleeping bags may be used to conserve as much heat as possible, with the two warmers lying on either side of the victim creating a "heat sandwich." Before the warmers get into the bag with the victim, they should exercise vigorously, both before attempting rewarming and afterwards to maintain their own temperatures. If enough people are available, the warmers should be relieved after approximately 30 minutes.
- Warm bath or shower (a bathtub is more desirable). This approach must be used only with a conscious vic-

A makeshift lean-to shelter and fire (at a distance) cuts down heat loss from wind while victim rewarms]

tim. Water should be approximately 70° and raised gradually to 110° after 10–20 minutes.

- Warm compresses. "Hot" water bottles (up to 110°) or towel-wrapped warm rocks can be placed next to the trunk of the victim.

15 There are a few other important items to remember when dealing with a hypothermia victim.

- Never leave the victim alone.
- Don't transport the victim if medical assistance can be brought to him or her. Transportation increases the likelihood of physical stress and shock.
- Never give alcoholic beverages to a hypothermia victim.
- The conscious victim should drink as much warm, sweet liquid as possible, including sugar and honey.
- Do not give the victim any medications such as painkillers, sedatives, aspirin, etc.
- Do not massage or jostle the victim.
- The victim should not smoke. Smoking curtails blood circulation to the hands, feet and skin.

- During rescue efforts, shield the victim from wind chill caused by boat, truck, snowmobile or other modes of transportation including down-drafts from helicopter rotors.

When the victim starts to sweat, it is a good indication that they are fully rewarmed and entering hyperthermia.

The Hypothermic Wrap

16 **The three main areas** of heat loss from the human body are the head, the armpits, and the groin. The hypothermic wrap is a quick and efficient method of covering these areas with only one blanket (although more may be employed if available). It has the advantage of leaving the arms and legs exposed so the pooled blood from these extremities is not drawn back to the heart triggering ventricular fibrillation.

17 David S. Smith, Ph.D., eminent water safety expert and lecturer, recommends the following procedures for wrapping the hypothermic victim:

The "hypothermic wrap" keeps heat concentrated on torso and head, leaving extremities uncovered. (Note elevated feet helping to keep cool blood from moving back toward heart.]

- Lay the victim diagonally across the prewarmed blanket on a flat surface. Place the top corner of the blanket over the victim's head to prevent further heat loss.
- Fold the left and right sides of the blanket horizontally over the trunk of the body.
- Pull the bottom corner of the blanket upwards over the groin area, and elevate feet slightly.

18 The primary consideration is to simply keep the victim from growing colder, not to totally rewarm or increase body temperature. Donating heat with hot packs (or wrapping warm rocks—110° maximum) applied to the torso and mouth-to-mouth breathing are usually sufficient to prevent further heat loss. Raising the victim off the ground with items such as blankets, air mattresses, etc., will also prevent body-heat loss to the ground.

Hypothermia Survival Times

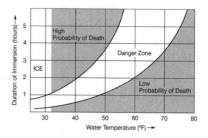

The Danger Zone indicates where safety precautions and appropriate behavior (adapting H.E.L.P.) can increase your chances of survival when immersed in cold water.

Levels of Hypothermia

Core Temperature (F°)	Symptoms
99.6	"Normal" rectal temperature
98.6	"Normal" oral temperature
96.8	Elevated metabolic rate
95.0	Maximum shivering
93.2	Victim still conscious and responsive
91.4	Severe hypothermia below this temperature
89.6	Consciousness clouded, pupils dilated, shivering stops
86.0	Progressive loss of consciousness, muscle rigidity increases, pulse and blood pressure difficult to obtain, breathing decreases
82.4	Ventricular fibrillation possible if heart irritated (by jostling victim or performing CPR)
80.6	Voluntary motion ceases, pupils nonreactive to light
78.8	Victim seldom conscious
77.0	Ventricular fibrillation may develop spontaneously
68.0	Heart standstill
64.4	Lowest accidental hypothermia victim to recover
48.2	Lowest artificially cooled hypothermia patient to recover

<u>Note</u>: These are generalizations—symptoms may vary from victim to victim.

Hypothermia and Cold Water near Drowning: Amazing Stories

19 **In May 1981,** a three-year-old girl was playing in her parents' backyard adjoining a lake near Alexandria [Minnesota]. Curious about the lake, the child wandered onto the dock and fell into the water. Fifteen minutes later, her father noticed she was missing. He found her floating face down under the dock and pulled her from the 40-plus degree water.

20 Responding to a call for help, a Douglas County Sheriff's deputy and his partner arrived on the scene in minutes. They found the young victim lying face-down in the backyard. They checked for signs of life, found none, and began cardiopulmonary resuscitation (CPR) immediately. An ambulance arrived from Alexandria. Emergency medical technicians relieved the deputy and his partner and the child was rushed to Douglas County Hospital. In the emergency room, the girl's heartbeat and breathing were restored. After that, her condition improved rapidly. Next day she was talking, and two days later, she left the hospital doing just fine.

21 Why was this rescue and recovery possible? We have all heard that someone under the water for five minutes suffers brain damage and death. The answer to the girl's recovery lies in a phenomenon known as the "Mammalian Diving Reflex." Hypothermia plays a significant role in the diving reflex by acting as a trigger for a series of complex bodily responses. Sudden facial contact with cold water causes a drop in pulse (to as few as two beats per minute) and constriction of the blood vessels. These conditions produce an increase in blood pressure. These reactions divert blood circulation away from the arms, legs and skin to the heart, lungs and brain, a process that can extend a victim's life for an amazingly long submersion. Hypothermia researcher Dr. Martin J. Nemiroff was personally involved in the successful rescue of a little girl who had been submerged for 60 minutes. The child, who had been involved in an accident in the icy waters off the coast of Alaska, made a complete recovery with no apparent brain damage.

Since young people cool down faster than adults, the diving reflex is more pronounced in infants and young children than it is with adults. The water must be colder than 70° for the reflex to be effectively produced.

22 If you encounter a victim who has been submerged in cold water for a relatively long period of time (60 minutes or less) and is not breathing, begin mouth-to-mouth resuscitation immediately—in the water if necessary. If you cannot detect a pulse, start CPR and summon medical assistance. If you are successful in reviving the victim, insist that he or she be examined

by a doctor. Often near-drowning victims that have been revived are embarrassed and want to go home. Unfortunately, these persons if untreated often die within 24 hours; they succumb from heart/lung and blood chemistry problems.

23 The victim's chances of recovery are better if they have "drowned" in clean, fresh water, than in salt water or stagnant ponds. This is related to the amount and type of impurities inhaled by the victim and the severity of infections they may cause.

Self-Rescue

24 **There are a number of things** you can do to help yourself if you fall overboard or capsize your boat. They will help delay the onset of hypothermia, prolong your survival time and improve your chances for rescue.

- **Get back in the boat!** The importance of reboarding your craft—even if it's filled with water—can't be over-emphasized. Most small boats if overturned, can be righted and bailed out. In fact, modern small craft have built-in flotation that will support the weight of the occupants, even after capsizing or swamping.

  If you can't right the boat, climb on top and hang on! Since children are smaller and generally have less body fat than adults, it is especially important to get them out of the water as soon as possible.

The U.S. Coast Guard recently completed a series of hypothermia studies in cold, rough water. These experiments confirmed earlier calm water tests showing that it is always preferable for a survivor to get out of the water and back onto an overturned boat. This was found to be true even in high winds. Cold water saps body heat 25 times faster than air of the same temperature and wind chill is not found to be a factor as long as the victim is clothed.

- **Keep your shirt on.** Almost all clothing, even hip boots and waders, will float for an extended period of time. As long as you remain calm and don't thrash about, air trapped within the fabric will hold a considerable amount of buoyancy.

- **While you still have them on,** your shirt or coat can be used as a flotation aid by buttoning them up to the collar and forcing air into them by blowing into the space between the top buttons and collar or by using the palm of your hand to splash air from the surface into the front of the garment at the bottom.

- **You won't die with your boots on.** Many hunters have died because they attempted to remove their boots when they fell in the water. What they didn't know was that, if they bent their legs, the air trapped in hip boots or waders could have kept them warm and afloat for hours. You should attempt to remove your clothing only if it is absolutely necessary and it is hampering your efforts to climb back into the boat.

- **Think or swim.** Do not attempt swimming, unless it is to a *nearby* boat or floating object. It has been shown that in 50° water a strong swimmer has only a 50/50 chance of reaching shore one-half mile away. Swimming, treading water, and survival floating (also known as drown-proofing) all use up valuable energy and greatly increase heat loss by pumping out any warm water trapped between layers of clothing and increasing the flow of cold water over the skin. As the heart beats faster, a greater volume of blood is circulated to the peripheral areas (limbs and skin). This speeds the transfer of heat to the water and quickens the onset of hypothermia.

  Studies have shown that 97 percent of all adult males can float motionlessly, hands stretched behind their heads, with faces out of the water for long periods. If large waves prevent floating on the back, an individual should keep his or her head out of the water and slowly tread water or dog paddle. The operative word here is *slowly*. Excess movement, such as swimming or thrashing about, accelerates heat loss and encourages hypothermia. Unconsciousness can occur in as little as 15 minutes in very cold water: death follows unconsciousness.

  If forced to swim in cold water, use strokes such as the breast stroke that keep your head out of the water. Strokes such as the crawl require swimmers to raise their arms out of the water. The weight of a raised arm (plus wet clothing) can force your head under. Since perhaps as much as 50 percent of heat is lost through the head, you can see why it is so important to keep it dry!

- **Wear your PFD.** A PFD increases your survival time in cold water in several ways: It decreases the amount of movement necessary to remain afloat, and it helps to insulate against heat loss. A personal flotation device will also keep you afloat if you become unconscious due to hypothermia.

  A Type II "horse-collar" device has little heat conserving value, where the Type III,

The "huddle" has three advantages: body heat is shared, it is easier for rescuers to spot a group than individuals floating, and morale is boosted by communication with others in group.

full-sleeved jacket models are much more heat efficient. The difference comes from the area covered by the device. If the high heat loss areas such as head, neck, sides, and groin areas are shielded, less heat will escape and survival is prolonged.

- **H.E.L.P. yourself.** If you fall in while wearing a PFD, decide not to swim for shore, and can't get back into your swamped boat, you can reduce the effects of hypothermia by assuming the heat-escape-lessening-position (H.E.L.P.). Begin by crossing your ankles, then cross your arms over your chest, draw your knees to your chest, lean back, and try to relax. This head-out-of-the-water, fetal position reduces body-heat flow to the water by at least 50 percent. It should, however, be tried in a pool with

the exact model of life jacket and the clothing you normally wear before depending on it, since it may be difficult or impossible to do with certain PFD types. Note that, if possible, the hands should be kept high on the shoulders or neck.

If kept out of the water, the hands will stay warmer and more flexible—an important factor in self-rescue.

If more than one person is in the water and all are wearing PFDs, the "huddle" is recommended. This is where small groups of two to four "hug" with chest closely touching chest. Your arms should be placed around the backs of the others. Smaller individuals or children can be placed in the middle of the "sandwich." The huddle helps to conserve body heat. It's also easier for rescuers to locate a huddle of victims than one lone survivor. The close proximity of victims can serve also as a significant morale booster.

Avoiding Hypothermia: The Iceman (Need not) Cometh

25 Most immersion hypothermia deaths involve non-PFD wearing victims that had no intention of entering the water. The obvious means to avoid hypothermia is to keep from falling into the water in the first place. However, if you do fall in, be ready to take immediate action to get out.

- Sit low in the boat. Don't stand or move around unless absolutely necessary. Many capsizings and falls overboard are due to the victim losing their balance or tripping over equipment in the boat.
- Don't overload. This is another common cause of capsizing and probably the number one cause of duck-hunter fatalities.
- Don't slow down too quickly. Sudden deceleration often allows the stern wake to overtake and swamp the boat by washing over the transom.
- Avoid alcoholic beverages. Drinking does not warm the body, but does tend to impair judgment, especially in an emergency situation.
- Wear your U.S. Coast Guard approved PFD, preferably a full coat

model that offers extended hypothermia protection.

- If you do capsize or fall out of your boat, get back in or climb on top. Do not attempt to swim to shore unless the boat has sunk.

Full body-covering immersion suits offer the ultimate in hypothermia protection.

Cold Water Survival

- Plan what you'll do if you fall in. Even in the coldest water . . . you don't have to die!
- Always wear a life jacket. It will help decrease the amount of movement you'll need to stay afloat.
- Get back in the boat. Your chances of survival are better—even if it's full of water.
- Avoid alcoholic beverages. They don't warm you up, and may cause you to make dumb mistakes that can be fatal in a cold water environment.
- Victims of all but the mildest cases of hypothermia should be treated by a doctor.

Acknowledgments

Our sincere thanks and appreciation to Robert S. Pozos, Ph.D., former director of the Hypothermia and Water Safety Laboratory at the University of Minnesota—Duluth. Much of the information in this publication comes from the excellent book he co-authored with David O. Born, Ph.D., entitled *Hypothermia: Causes, Effects, Prevention* (New Century Publishers, Inc., Piscataway, NJ, copyright 1982).

The "hypothermic wrap" was initiated by the U.S. Coast Guard Boating Safety Detachment in Portsmouth, Virginia, headed by Chief Warrant Officer Lonnie Hyatt, and was excerpted from the book *Water Wise* by David S. Smith, Ph.D., and Sara J. Smith.

Hypothermia . . . The Cold Facts, written by Timothy M. Smalley, boating safety specialist, Minnesota Department of Natural Resources. Design, layout and photographs by the author.

Post-Reading

Basic Comprehension

MULTIPLE CHOICE

Circle the choice that best answers each question.

1. Which is NOT true of hypothermia?

    a. Cold-water-immersion hypothermia usually happens more quickly than cold-air hypothermia.

    b. Cold-water-immersion hypothermia won't be fatal if a person can keep from drowning.

    c. How quickly hypothermia occurs varies from person to person.

    d. Slight hypothermic states are common and not particularly harmful.

2. Alcohol affects the brain by_____.

    a. preventing vasodilation

    b. reducing oxygen supply

    c. increasing shivering

    d. improving memory

3. Which of the following can be inferred from the discussion of shivering in Paragraph 6?

    a. About 10 percent of the population is particularly resistant to hypothermia.

    b. The shiver reflex does not require signals from the brain to be activated.

    c. Shivering produces an insignificant amount of heat that rarely helps protect the body.

    d. People with no shiver reflex are at greater risk of hypothermia than others.

4. According to the first sentence in Paragraph 9, "cooling rates for various individuals vary for the reasons discussed earlier." Which statement expresses the "reasons" this sentence refers to?

   a. "age, weight, sex, physical and mental condition of the victim, water temperature, amount and type of clothing being worn, whether or not the victim is wearing a personal flotation device (PFD), and if the victim remains motionless, thrashes about, or tries to swim"

   b. "increases in blood pressure, heart rate, and adrenaline levels"

   c. "'mental toughness' and a positive attitude about your survival and rescue will extend your survival time."

   d. "the bizarre physical and psychological changes often brought about by intoxication [which] impair short-term and long-term memory and inhibit an individual's ability to act in an appropriate manner to help themselves in an emergency situation"

5. According to the reading, a metalized fabric space blanket _____.

   a. is just as effective as body-to-body rewarming

   b. slows a victim's rate of recovery

   c. increases the effectiveness of body-to-body rewarming

   d. can be used as a PDF

6. According to the reading, which statement is true about the process of rewarming hypothermia victims?

   a. Unconscious victims should be warmed in a bathtub if one is available.

   b. Wet clothing should not be removed.

   c. Victims should avoid air or water that feels warm to the touch.

   d. Some movement can help the victim recover faster.

7. According to the table on page 99, which statement correctly matches a body core temperature to the onset (starting point) of a physical condition?

   a. 89.6 degrees Fahrenheit—The victim stops thinking clearly.

   b. 68.0 degrees Fahrenheit—The victim's heart becomes vulnerable to serious damage.

   c. 95.0 degrees Fahrenheit—The victim can no longer move any part of his or her body.

   d. 91.4 degrees Fahrenheit—The victim's eyes stop responding to bright light.

8. What can be most strongly inferred from the reading about the Mammalian Diving Reflex?

   a. It includes the Torso Reflex.
   b. It is less likely to occur in a person who falls backwards into water than in one who falls frontwards.
   c. It does not occur in adults.
   d. It is less likely to occur in a person who jumps into the water than in one who falls.

9. Which is NOT presented in the reading as a reason to avoid swimming long distances in cold water?

   a. Swimming causes more cold water to touch the skin.
   b. Swimming reduces the flow of oxygen to the brain.
   c. Swimming uses energy that is needed to maintain core temperature.
   d. Swimming reduces the amount of warm water trapped near the skin.

10. For which TWO reasons is the breast stroke recommended to people who must swim in cold water?

    a. It allows them to keep their heads out of water.
    b. It helps them reach their targets quickly.
    c. It keeps their arms underwater.
    d. It uses little energy.

TRUE OR FALSE

Circle T if the statement is true according to the reading or F if the statement is false.

T F 1. If you know you're about to fall into cold water, you should put your hands over your face.

T F 2. If your boat overturns and there are high winds, it's better to stay in the water than to get on the boat.

T F 3. If you fall in cold water, remove heavy clothes and boots.

T F 4. Even if you're far from shore, you should swim or tread water so you keep moving.

T F 5. A hypothermia victim should always see a doctor even if the victim revives and feels fine.

T F 6. If you notice that a person has symptoms of hypothermia, you should start rewarming them without delay.

T F 7. If a shelter is too small for much movement, a conscious hypothermia victim should leave the shelter and move around.

T F 8. It's fine for a hypothermia victim to take aspirin to relieve pain.

T F 9. Young children cool down faster than adults.

SHORT ANSWER

Rewrite the false sentences to make them true.

_____

_____

_____

_____

_____

Vocabulary

NEAR SYNONYMS

Cross out the word or phrase in parentheses that is most different in meaning from the others. Then write an original sentence in your own words using each crossed-out word appropriately.

1. If your boat (capsizes/overturns/pitches), try to get out of the water and on top of it, even if there's a strong wind.

   _____

   _____

   _____

2. It is most important to retain heat in the head and the (limbs/torso/trunk), so concentrate on insulating these parts of the body.

   _____

   _____

   _____

3. Drinking increases the (dangers/hazards/symptoms) of boating on cold water.

   _____

   _____

   _____

4. Victims of hypothermia may exhibit (noticeable/pronounced/slight) differences from their normal personalities.

   _____

   _____

   _____

5. Suddenly falling into cold water can (induce/trigger/impair) gasping.

   _____

   _____

   _____

PARAPHRASING

Using the best key vocabulary item from the list, rephrase each of the statements. Change as much of the original as necessary to use the item you have chosen, but do not change the meaning of the original. Use each item from the list only once

deceleration	proximity	revive	succumb
indication	retain	stalwart	vigorous

1. When the body cannot maintain its core temperature in a cold environment, it is overwhelmed by the effects of hypothermia.

   _____

   _____

   _____

2. If you fall into cold water, don't remove your clothes—they help to keep heat in.

   _____

   _____

   _____

3. The decision as to whether or not you should swim for land depends on how close you are to it.

   _____

   _____

   _____

4. Although energetic exercise can warm the body on land, swimming in cold water can use up energy and actually lead to a decrease in body temperature.

   _____

   _____

   _____

5. Even the bravest swimmer can panic when unexpectedly plunged into cold water.

_____

_____

_____

6. Sudden changes to an individual's personality can be a sign of hypothermia.

_____

_____

_____

7. If you slow down a boat too quickly, it can lead to an accident.

_____

_____

_____

8. Alcohol should not be used to try to bring a hypothermia victim around because not only does it not actually warm the body but it also contributes to preventing warming.

_____

_____

_____

MULTIPLE CHOICE

Choose the word or phrase closest in meaning to the italicized word in each sentence from the reading.

1. "Although the accident report officially listed the cause of death as drowning, chances are the victim succumbed to an *insidious* killer that is involved in as many as perhaps 50 percent of all boating deaths: hypothermia."

   a. hidden and harmful
   b. powerful and violent
   c. related
   d. unrecognized

2. "Do not massage or *jostle* the victim."

   a. excite
   b. overheat
   c. rub
   d. shake

3. "In May 1981, a three-year-old girl was playing in her parents' backyard *adjoining* a lake near Alexandria [Minnesota]."

   a. across from
   b. in sight of
   c. next to
   d. surrounded by

4. "Sudden facial contact with cold water causes a drop in pulse (to as few as two beats per minute) and *constriction* of the blood vessels."

   a. cooling
   b. loss of control
   c. reaction
   d. tightening

5. "The victim's chances of recovery are better if they have 'drowned' in clean, fresh water, than in salt water or *stagnant* ponds."

   a. inland
   b. not flowing
   c. not natural
   d. small

6. "This is related to the amount and type of *impurities* inhaled by the victim and the severity of infections they may cause."

   a. bacteria
   b. defects
   c. contaminants
   d. liquid

7. "This is related to the amount and type of impurities *inhaled* by the victim and the severity of infections they may cause."

   a. absorbed
   b. breathed in
   c. met with
   d. swallowed

8. "As long as you remain calm and don't *thrash about*, air trapped within the fabric will hold a considerable amount of buoyancy."

   a. move wildly
   b. panic
   c. sink
   d. swim quickly

Reading Focus

Formal Verbs

MATCHING

In academic writing, certain formal verbs may be preferred over more common verbs that have similar meanings. Match the formal verbs on the left with less formal verbs on the right that have a similar meaning.

1. conduct _____   a. do

2. determine _____   b. cause

3. assume _____   c. figure out

4. induce _____   d. give

5. render _____   e. take

Collocations

MATCHING

Write the nouns from the list next to the verbs with which they are commonly used. Each verb can be used with more than one noun. Some nouns can be used with more than one verb.

a cause   a position   an appearance
a limit   a reason   (e.g., a look of
a maximum   a reflex (e.g. gasping)   innocence)
a minimum   a service   an effect
a physical condition   a study   an experiment
   (e.g. vasodilation   a survey   assistance
   or drowsiness)   aid   research
a poll

1. You can conduct _____.

2. You can determine _____.

3. You can assume _____.

4. You can induce _____.

5. You can render _____.

Integrating Information

ANNOTATING TEXT

Skim the reading again. Make notes in the margin to identify each occurrence from the list. Some appear in more than one place. When you finish, compare answers in a small group.

   isolated facts (or lists of facts) about hypothermia

   true stories about hypothermia

   explanations of technical terms or definitions

   biological explanations

   isolated tips (or lists of tips) on avoiding or surviving hypothermia

   elaborated tips on avoiding or surviving hypothermia

Putting Reading to Work

COMPOSING A PAMPHLET

In a small group, choose an area with an extreme environment where people go for outdoor activities, such as Death Valley National Park or Mount Everest. Collaborate to write a pamphlet similar to *Hypothermia . . . The Cold Facts*. It should aim to help visitors survive the extreme environment. Your pamphlet should include descriptions of the dangers to avoid, explanations of how the human body reacts to the environment, tips on avoiding the dangers, and suggestions for maximizing chances of survival if visitors do suffer from problems. Illustrate your points with true stories of survival and of death caused by the environment. Use the readings in this chapter and outside resources to find facts, survival tips, and true stories, but write the pamphlet in your own words.

The Airline Business

One of the largest and most complicated parts of the U.S. economy is the air-travel sector. This unit is about the difficult but vital business of running airlines and an air-travel system. The unit is organized as follows:

- FIRST TIER: The Hub-and-Spoke System
  1. Introductory passage: **The Hub-and-Spoke System**
  2. Journal article: **Air Transportation: Deregulation and Its Consequences** by Assif Siddiqi

- SECOND TIER: Big Versus Small
  Commentary: **No Size Fits**

- THIRD TIER: Scalability
  Journal article: **Scalability and Evolutionary Dynamics of Air Transportation Networks in the United States** by Philippe A. Bonnefoy and R. John Hansman, Jr.

First Tier: The Hub-and-Spoke System

Pre-Reading

DISCUSSION

This reading discusses a type of system some airlines use to route many passengers through an extra city before they arrive at their final destination. Before you read, discuss the questions in a small group. Use a dictionary and other reference sources as necessary.

1. Think about the most recent trip you've taken on a plane. What was your starting city? What was your destination city? Did your itinerary require you to change planes in a city between your starting point and your final destination?

2. What type of shops and restaurants were at the different airports you visited? Why do you think they are similar or different?

3. Do you prefer to fly in smaller planes or larger planes? Why?

Reading

The Hub-and-Spoke System

1 Air connections in the United States (and other countries) are built on a "hub-and-spoke" model. For each airline, certain airports operate as centers (hubs) for travel on their routes. Other, smaller cities are "spoke" cities. They connect to at least one hub but usually not to each other. Very few flights (or none at all) go from spoke to spoke without first passing through a hub that the spokes share.

2 Let us illustrate this with a fictional example. Imagine you want to fly on Sparrow Airlines from Cleveland, Ohio, to Savannah, Georgia. The trip is not very long, but you have to go far out of your way to complete it. Cleveland and Savannah are small-market spoke cities for Sparrow Air, so there are no direct flights between them. From Cleveland, you might fly to Memphis, which is a hub. This hub is shared by both the Cleveland spoke and the Savannah spoke. You fly into the hub on the Cleveland spoke. You then fly out of the hub along the Savannah spoke and reach your destination.

3 The logic behind a hub-and-spoke system is strong. Because there are few people who want to fly to Savannah from Cleveland, it makes

sense to bring the Cleveland plane to Memphis, let it fill with passengers from other smaller cities around the region, and then continue on with a full flight to Savannah. The airline spends less money because it flies fuller planes. Also, the airline does not have to keep full maintenance or service crews at every airport in its network. Small staffs take care of the smaller "spoke" airports, while full maintenance, public relations, and administrative services are concentrated in the hubs.

4 Also, the needs of a large group of customers, travelers whose destination is the hub, are well met. Because hub cities are relatively large centers of business, travelers are much more likely to have a hub city as their destination than to aim for any particular spoke city. Hub airports, then, can support an attractive array of shops and restaurants because the customer base is there. With extensive rent-a-car and shuttle services at every hub airport, travelers with hub destinations can easily get to town and get to work. Spreading these resources throughout a system of small airports would result in mediocre service for everyone. Concentrating them in a few hubs provides good service to the majority of travelers, even if some passengers must settle for a lower level of service at outlying airports.

5 Since the mid-1950s, this system has functioned well enough—at least from the airlines' point of view—but its usefulness may be nearing an end. Hub airports are becoming so uncomfortable for passengers that increasing numbers of potential air travelers are staying away. The flying public is losing patience with long waiting lines at nearly every stage of the flying experience—at check-in desks, at security checkpoints, on runways, and at freeway entrance ramps near the airport. These are the inevitable results of funneling more people through the same chokepoints. At the same time, they fear security problems at such big airports, where confusion could allow terrorists to slip through the system.

6 Another problem with a hub-and-spoke system is that hub cities are far too important to the system as a whole. Hubs like Minneapolis, Chicago, Denver, and Boston are frequently slowed by bad weather, especially in winter. A traveler in Iowa may see great weather, perfect for a flight to sunny Phoenix. However, the flight is scheduled to pass through the Minneapolis hub, which has shut down for at least 12 hours because of a blizzard. Minneapolis's weather—or Chicago's or some other hub's—has become a problem for travelers only because they have to pass through a hub.

7 Some remedies are being tried. New, small airlines have begun operating from spoke city to spoke city, avoiding the congestion problems at hubs. They usually fly from small-city airports where systems are dependable but not overloaded.

8 Air-travel enthusiasts are also trying to revitalize the nearly 5,000 U.S. airports that now handle only very few regularly scheduled commercial flights (or, in many cases, none at all). The airport in St. Cloud, Minnesota, about 60 miles northwest of the Twin Cities, is a good example. It is small but in good repair. Its runways are long enough to handle all but the very largest commercial jets, and it is located in a high-demand area. Regular service out of St. Cloud to, say, Willow Run near Detroit, Michigan, would bring passengers within business reach of the big cities (Detroit and Minneapolis-St. Paul) without the lines, the confusion, and other inconveniences of hub airports.

9 Even more-visionary schemes assume a fleet of small, new planes that are almost crash-proof. Only one or two people would ride in one of these mini-planes. This may sound like the present-day private jet, but it would be far cheaper and far easier for a modestly trained pilot to fly. Some prototypes are for airplanes that will float to the ground on a parachute if a problem occurs. Such design features would never work on large commercial jets, only on smaller planes. The new small-scale aviation wave, then, may bring safer travel along with far greater flexibility for air travelers.

References

AirNav, LLC, "St. Cloud Regional Airport." Accessed at www.airnav.com. February 15, 2006.

Fallows, James. "Air Travel's Next Generation." Speech to The Commonwealth Club, August 6, 2001. Transcript accessed at www.commonwealth club.org/archive March 3, 2006.

Post-Reading

Basic Comprehension

MULTIPLE CHOICE

Circle the choice that best answers each question.

1. Which best expresses the main idea of the reading?

   a. New, safe private planes will make the hub-and-spoke system unnecessary.

   b. Problems with the hub-and-spoke system have led people to look for alternatives.

   c. The hub-and-spoke system allows flights directly from one spoke to another.

   d. The hub-and-spoke system is the most practical way for airlines to organize their service.

2. According to the reading, why are hubs beneficial to travelers?

   a. They are a necessary part of the air-travel system.

   b. They are the ultimate destination for some travelers.

   c. They encourage airlines to have full service crews in spoke cities.

   d. They provide extensive services to a majority of customers.

3. The reading implies that which one would suffer if the hub-and-spoke system faded and a spoke-to-spoke system became common?

   a. big airlines

   b. big cities

   c. small airlines

   d. small cities

4. Which is NOT discussed in the reading as an area of difference between the hub-and-spoke system and newer systems being developed?

   a. the amount of time spent waiting in lines

   b. the dependability of services

   c. the difficulty of reaching major cities

   d. the safety of runways

5. Which of the following is NOT mentioned in the reading as a reason some travelers dislike hub airports?

   a. Travelers are often delayed because of too few planes.

   b. Travelers face heavy traffic on the roads near airports.

   c. Travelers must wait in long lines for airport services.

   d. Travelers worry that terrorists will focus on large airports.

6. Why does the traveler in Iowa mentioned in Paragraph 6 have a problem?

   a. A snowstorm in Minneapolis is moving toward Iowa.

   b. The plane he should be on is stuck in a snowstorm.

   c. There is a snowstorm in a hub city.

   d. There is a snowstorm in a spoke city.

7. According to Paragraph 8, what do 5,000 airports have in common?

   a. They are not in very good repair.

   b. They are not used as much as they could be.

   c. They are not used for commercial air service.

   d. They are small, but near big cities.

8. Why might new "mini-planes" be safer than present-day private jets?

   a. Certain design features make crashes very unlikely.

   b. Even a modestly trained pilot can fly them.

   c. Their design features could never work on large jets.

   d. They are smaller.

Vocabulary

MATCHING

Match the word or phrase on the left with the one on the right that most closely relates to it.

1. something with a *hub* and *spokes* (Paragraph 1) _____

2. something that can *connect* other things (Paragraph 1) _____

3. *taking care of* something (Paragraph 3) _____

4. the *flying public* (Paragraph 5) _____

5. a *funnel* (Paragraph 5) _____

6. something that could be a *chokepoint* (Paragraph 5) _____

7. one kind of *remedy* (Paragraph 7) _____

8. *revitalization* (Paragraph 8) _____

9. a *crash* (Paragraph 9) _____

10. what a *wave* is like (Paragraph 9) _____

a. an accident

b. a bicycle wheel

c. a simple device for pouring liquids through a narrow opening

d. bringing back to life

e. a chain

f. medicine

g. a moving "hill" of water

h. a narrow passage

i. travelers

j. providing what is needed

Reading Focus

SCHEMATIC TABLE

Information from the reading can be sorted into two categories. The list of nine items contains statements that, according to the reading, fit into one of the categories. Arrange the characteristics into one of two categories. TWO of the statements will not be used.

airlines can concentrate staff in big cities

almost no spoke-to-spoke travel

every plane is protected with a parachute

fewer inefficient, half-filled flights

higher number of small planes in operation

lessens the region-wide impact of bad weather at a hub

many different combinations of flights to and from smaller cities possible

relatively less crowded airports

requires massive rebuilding of airport runways

Characteristics of a Hub-and-Spoke System	Characteristics of Alternative Systems

Integrating Information

PLACE REFERENCES

On the map, mark the places listed. Use a dot to show each location and label each place by name. Consult outside reference sources (e.g., an atlas, a geographical dictionary, a map-oriented website) if necessary.

Boston, Massachusetts
Chicago, Illinois
Cleveland, Ohio
Dayton, Ohio
Denver, Colorado
Detroit, Michigan
Iowa

Memphis, Tennessee
Minneapolis, Minnesota
Phoenix, Arizona
St. Cloud Airport
Savannah, Georgia
Willow Run Airport

SUMMARIZING

Answer the questions in your own words.

1. In what ways is a hub-and-spoke system good for business?

   _____

   _____

   _____

2. In what ways is a hub-and-spoke system bad for business?

   _____

   _____

   _____

SYNTHESIZING

Think about your own experience at airports and answer the questions based on what you read and what you have experienced.

1. Describe a large airport you have traveled through. Include a detail or an example in each answer to make it more interesting. Comment on other characteristics of the airport that you remember.

   How busy was it? _____

   _____

   Did it have any shops or services in the terminal? _____

   _____

   Did you wait a long time to check in for your flight? _____

   _____

   Did you wait a long time to get your luggage checked by security crews? _____

   _____

   Were you worried about criminal activity (e.g., someone stealing your luggage)? _____

   _____

Were you worried about a terrorist attack? _____

_____

Other comments: _____

_____

_____

2. Describe a small airport you have traveled through. Include a detail or example in each answer to make it more interesting. Comment on other characteristics of the airport that you remember.

How busy was it? _____

Did it have any shops or services in the terminal? _____

Did you wait a long time to check in for your flight? _____

Did you wait a long time to get your luggage checked by security crews? _____

Were you worried about criminal activity (e.g., someone stealing your luggage)? _____

Were you worried about a terrorist attack? _____

Other comments: _____

_____

3. Compare your descriptions. Write a short essay (3–4 paragraphs) contrasting the two airports. Alternatively, you could give an oral presentation (about five minutes).

Pre-Reading

DISCUSSION

This reading discusses the Civil Aeronautics Board and regulation and deregulation of the aviation industry. Before you read, discuss the questions in a small group. Use a dictionary and other reference sources as necessary.

1. What person or group do you think should be in charge of regulating the airlines?

2. Over what do you think the regulators should have control? Fares? Routes? Schedules? Other things?

3. Do you think more or fewer regulations are needed in today's air transportation? Why do you think so?

Reading

Air Transportation:
Deregulation and Its Consequences

1 Until 1978, the U.S. government, through the Civil Aeronautics Board (CAB), regulated many areas of commercial aviation such as fares, routes, and schedules. The Airline Deregulation Act of 1978, however, removed many of these controls, thus changing the face of civil aviation in the United States. After deregulation, unfettered free competition ushered in a new era in passenger air travel.

2 The CAB had three main functions: to award routes to airlines, to limit the entry of air carriers into new markets, and to regulate fares for passengers. Much of the established practices of commercial passenger travel within the United States, however, went back even farther, to the policies of Walter Folger Brown, the U.S. postmaster general in the 1920s and early 1930s in the administration of President Herbert Hoover. Brown had changed the mail payments system to encourage the manufacture of passenger aircraft instead of mail-carrying aircraft. His influence was crucial in awarding contracts so as to create four major domestic airlines: United, American, Eastern, and Transcontinental and Western Air (TWA). Similarly, Brown had also helped give Pan American a monopoly on international routes.

3 The Civil Aeronautics Act of 1938 put in place a regulatory organization, known after 1940 as the Civil Aeronautics Board, that was authorized to not only supervise the air transport industry, but

also to promote and develop it. The goals of the CAB were to provide the American public with the safest, most efficient, least expensive, and widest-ranging air service possible. The CAB accomplished these objectives by regulating such aspects of the commercial aviation sector as entry into and exit from individual markets (by dictating the route patterns between cities and the frequency of flights), fares for passengers and cargo, safety, financing, subsidies to carriers flying on less profitable routes, mergers and acquisitions, inter-carrier agreements, and the quality of service. Proponents of regulation claimed that the CAB used its power appropriately to mandate carriers to fly routes of high traffic volume (and therefore high profit) as well as those with low traffic and profit. Without regulation, advocates argued, the airlines would concentrate on flying high volume and high profit routes, depriving out-of-the-way communities of air transport altogether. Moreover, concentration of airlines on lucrative routes could easily create a business climate of cutthroat competition. In the process, the carriers would undercut the economic stability of the industry and possibly cut corners on safety and maintenance of aircraft in an effort to reduce costs to compete more effectively with the other carriers. It was the fear of cutthroat competition that had motivated Depression-era members of Congress to

vote for the Civil Aeronautics Act of 1938. Regulation also ensured that no one company could dominate the market in a particular region and thus be in a position to set high fares because of the lack of competition. Federal regulation was one way of assuring that the industry operated efficiently and with the greatest good for the greatest number of Americans, although perhaps at the price of subverting the free market.

4 The railroad industry in the latter half of the 19th century had earlier experienced each of the problems advocates of airline regulation wanted to guard against. Vertical integration by such men as Jay Gould had enabled control of markets between two points, with disastrous consequences for consumers to whom he could charge anything he wanted. Rate wars between competing railroads had also wrecked companies, with a long slow climb out of receivership following. Piecemeal attacks on these problems from various state legislatures created a patchwork quilt of regulations that varied from jurisdiction to jurisdiction, but since the problems were inherently interstate in focus, these efforts failed to bring resolution. The consequence was that by the 1880s many officials of both the railroad industry and the federal government were advocating national regulation to bring order to the chaos. It came with the creation of the Interstate Commerce Commission

in 1887 and found refinement thereafter. Air transportation offered essentially the same challenges and resolutions posed by the railroads a half century earlier.

5 Among the CAB's functions, one of the most important was to pick airlines from the available pool for a particular route rather than let the market decide which airline should fly that route. Established carriers already serving a route would usually evaluate new applicants and often found that the applicant lacked some requirement for flying an already-covered route. Thus, new entrants into the business were at a great disadvantage and were often shut out of key routes since the established airlines did not want new competition. Fare-setting also involved a similarly long process. In the airline industry, there was a general level of discontent about the laws that regulated civil aviation. Furthermore, discussions in Congress highlighted the fact that fares for routes within states were often much lower than fares between states, even if the actual routes were the exact same distance. This was partly because national routes were regulated to a much stricter degree than flights within states.

6 The push to deregulate, or at least to reform the existing laws governing passenger carriers, was accelerated by President Jimmy Carter, who appointed economist and former professor Alfred Kahn, a vocal supporter of deregulation, to head the CAB. A second force to deregulate emerged from abroad. In 1977, Freddie Laker, a British entrepreneur who owned Laker Airways, created the Skytrain service, which offered extraordinarily cheap fares for transatlantic flights. Laker's offerings coincided with a boom in low-cost domestic flights as the CAB eased some limitations on charter flights, i.e., flights offered by companies that do not actually own planes but leased them from the major airlines. The big air carriers responded by proposing their own lower fares. For example, American Airlines, the country's second largest airline, obtained CAB approval for "Super-Saver" tickets.

7 All of these events proved to be favorable for large-scale deregulation. In November 1977, Congress formally deregulated air cargo. In late 1978, Congress passed the Airline Deregulation Act of 1978, legislation that had been principally authored by Senators Edward Kennedy and Howard Cannon. There was stiff opposition to the bill—from the major airlines who feared free competition, from labor unions who feared nonunion employees, and from safety advocates who feared that safety would be sacrificed. Public support was, however, strong enough to pass the Act. The Act appeased the major airlines by offering generous subsidies and it pleased workers by offering high unemployment benefits if

they lost their jobs as a result. The most important effect of the Act, whose laws were slowly phased in, was on the passenger market. For the first time in 40 years, airlines could enter the market or (from 1981) expand their routes as they saw fit. Airlines (from 1982) also had full freedom to set their fares. In 1984, the CAB was finally abolished since its primary duty, that of regulating the airline industry, was no longer necessary.

8 What effect did deregulation have in the short term? First, many airlines abandoned less profitable routes that took passengers to smaller cities. For example, until 1978, United Airlines had flown to Bakersfield, California, a booming oil town of 225,000 people. With deregulation, United pulled out of Bakersfield, depriving the city of any flights to bigger cities such as San Francisco or Las Vegas. A second and related effect was the growth of "hub-and-spoke" routes. The major airlines "adopted" key cities as centers for their operations; these key cities served as stops for most flights, even if they were not on a direct route between two other end points. Delta Air Lines had a major hub at Atlanta while Eastern ran its hub operations from Miami. Both airlines ran many daily roundtrip flights from their hubs, thus keeping planes in the air for more hours each day and filling more seats. For example, the number of daily non-stop flights between New York and West Palm Beach, Florida, jumped from five to 23.

9 Third, deregulation allowed new start-up airlines to enter the market without having to agree to the demands of the larger established airlines. One of these was People's Express, founded by Donald Burr, a shrewd entrepreneur who introduced unconventional methods of management such as low salaries, fewer managers, employees who could perform multiple jobs, and equitable stock ownership by all employees. Burr ran an extremely tight operation where passengers had to pay for meals on planes and were charged for checked-in baggage. Fares were so low that they were comparable to intercity bus lines. People's Express revenues increased dramatically through the early 1980s, reaching a billion dollars by 1985. Eventually, though, People's couldn't compete with established airlines that also cut their prices but offered significantly better service. The older airlines, being linked with travel agents, also offered the option of advance ticket purchases. Within a year of reaching its peak, in 1986, Burr had to sell People's Express in the wake of rising losses and passenger dissatisfaction.

10 In general, freed from the rules of the CAB, regional and major airlines inaugurated new routes in droves. Airlines competed in a no-holds-barred competition for passenger business. As a

result, fares dropped dramatically and total operating revenues for the major national and international airlines rose to a high in 1979. The same year was also the peak year for passengers: an unprecedented 317 million passengers flew through American skies.

11 Unfortunately for the airline industry, fuel costs, economic recession, and wanton overexpansion in the wake of deregulation began to have serious negative consequences. The airlines recorded a net operating loss of $421 million as early as 1981, when the number of passengers fell to 286 million. The problems were worsened by the nationwide strike of the Professional Air Traffic Controllers Organization (PATCO) in 1981. One airline, Braniff, collapsed completely in 1982 (although the airline operated from 1984 under new ownership before entering bankruptcy once again in 1989). Other airlines continued to expand in the face of economic problems, putting them at great risk.

12 Analysts continue to debate the long-term effects of deregulation. The climate in the post-deregulation era was extremely unstable as illustrated by the fates of both Continental and Eastern Airlines, two major domestic carriers. Both airlines suffered through severe financial crises, which were made worse by mismanagement and bad relationships with the labor unions. Both ended up bankrupt by 1989. The most important international carrier for the United States, Pan American, suffered the same fate. Without the cover of regulation on international flights, Pan Am suddenly had to compete with new entrants such as Laker and People's Express. By the end of 1991, after a dramatic downfall through the 1980s, Pan Am was history. The number of major carriers in the United States fell from six in 1978—United, American, Delta, Eastern, TWA, and Pan Am—to three by 1991—United, American, and Delta. Ultimately, most of the big airlines suffered some sort of loss in the 1980s—either facing complete bankruptcy or with less financial growth than hoped.

13 There were some positive consequences of deregulation. The average airfare, for example, dropped by more than one-third between 1977 and 1992 (adjusting for inflation). It is estimated that ticket buyers saved as much as $100 billion on fares alone. Deregulation also allowed the proliferation of smaller airlines that took overthe shorter routes that were no longer profitable for the big carriers. In sum, the major airlines probably suffered the negative consequences of deregulation the most. New smaller airlines and the millions of passengers flying gained the most.

References

Bilstein, Roger. *Flight in America: From the Wrights to the Astronauts*, Rev. ed. Baltimore: The Johns Hopkins University Press, 1994.

Davies, R.E.G. *Airlines of the United States Since 1914*. Washington, D.C.: Smithsonian Institution Press, 1972.

Heppenheimer, T. A. *Turbulent Skies: The History of Commercial Aviation*. New York: John Wiley & Sons, 1995.

Online References

"Aviation Resource—History—1950–Present," http://www.geo cities.com/CapeCanaveral/4294/ history/1950_present.html.

Additional References

Bailey, Elizabeth E., Graham, David R., and Kaplan, Daniel P. *Deregulating the Airlines*. Cambridge, Mass.: The MIT Press, 1985.

Banks, Howard. *The Rise and Fall of Freddie Laker*. London: Faber & Faber, 1982.

Brenner, Melvin A., Leet, James O., and Schott, Elihu. *Airline Deregulation*. Westport, Conn.: Eno Foundation for Transportation, Inc. 1985.

Dempsey, Paul. *The Social and Economic Consequences of Deregulation*. Westport, Conn.: Quorum Books, 1989.

O'Connor, William E. *An Introduction to Airline Economics*, Fifth Edition. Westport, Conn.: Praeger, 1995.

Wyckoff, D. Daryl, and Maister, David H. *The Domestic Airline Industry*. Lexington, Mass.: D.C. Heath and Co., 1977

Post-Reading

Basic Comprehension

MULTIPLE CHOICE

Circle the choice that best answers each question.

1. During which time period did a group called the Civil Aeronautics Board (CAB) exist?

    a. 1940–1984
    b. 1938–1978
    c. 1940–1978
    d. 1940–1984

2. According to the reading, who is responsible for the fact that there were only four major domestic carriers in the 1930s?

    a. Herbert Hoover
    b. PanAmerican Airlines
    c. the CAB
    d. Walter Folger Brown

3. Before the CAB was founded, policy makers worried that too much competitive freedom for airlines would lead to _____.

    a. foreign control of the U.S. market
    b. high fares
    c. low fares
    d. too many carriers

4. Supporters of the former CAB said that it helped airlines serve a wide base of the public by _____.

    a. allowing airlines to set higher fares for low-profit routes
    b. assigning certain carriers to serve low-volume routes
    c. encouraging airlines to fly only high-traffic routes
    d. letting the market decide which airline should serve a certain city

5. Which of the following is NOT mentioned in the reading as a short-term effect of deregulation?

   a. Travelers lost faith in the government's ability to protect them.
   b. Connections to small cities were cancelled.
   c. The hub-and-spoke system came into place.
   d. New airlines could more easily start up.

6. According to the reading, the airline industry went from making a lot of money in the late 1970s to experiencing financial trouble in the early 1980s. Which of the following is mentioned as one cause of this reversal?

   a. a series of airplane crashes
   b. an increase in government regulations
   c. rises in the price of oil
   d. unrest in the Middle East

CHRONOLOGY

Arrange the events in historical order with 1 being the first thing to happen and 8 being the last.

_____ United Airlines cancels service to Bakersfield, California.

_____ Freddie Laker creates an airline offering extremely low fares.

_____ Four major domestic airlines are created.

_____ Pan American Airlines goes out of business.

_____ The airlines record a net operating loss of $421 million.

_____ The Civil Aeronautics Board is created.

_____ The Interstate Commerce Commission is created.

_____ Vertical integration of the railroad industry occurs.

Vocabulary

MULTIPLE CHOICE

Choose the word or phrase closest in meaning to the italicized words used in the reading.

1. Which of the following is closest in meaning to *regulation* (Paragraph 3)?

   a. measurements
   b. control
   c. customers
   d. equality

2. Which of the following is closest in meaning to *posed?* (Paragraph 4)

   a. challenged
   b. pretended
   c. positioned
   d. presented

3. Which of the following is closest in meaning to *pool?* (Paragraph 5)

   a. a group of persons or things
   b. a kind of game
   c. a person with power and influence
   d. a small body of water

4. Which of the following is closest in meaning to *shut out of?* (Paragraph 5)

   a. complained about
   b. disappointed by
   c. excluded from
   d. protected from

5. Which of the following is closest in meaning to *coincided with?* (Paragraph 6)

   a. occurred at the same time as
   b. resulted from
   c. started out as
   d. were intended to be

6. Which of the following is closest in meaning to *abolished?* (Paragraph 7)

   a. eliminated
   b. embarrassed
   c. established
   d. extended

7. Which of the following is closest in meaning to *unconventional?* (Paragraph 9)

   a. difficult
   b. isolated
   c. unpopular
   d. unusual

8. Which of the following is closest in meaning to *strike?* (Paragraph 11)

   a. missed opportunity
   b. political campaign
   c. refusal to work
   d. surprise attack

9. Which of the following is closest in meaning to *fate?* (Paragraph 12)

   a. how a company is structured
   b. what eventually happens to a company
   c. when a company goes through difficult times
   d. where a company's money comes from

PARAPHRASING

Using the best key vocabulary item from the list, rephrase the statements. Change as much of the original as necessary to use the item you have chosen, but do not change the meaning. Use each item from the list only once.

accelerate	cut corners	financing	phase in	undercut
altogether	ensure	large-scale	stable	usher in

1. Excellent marketing made it certain that the new video game would sell well.

   _____

   _____

2. Most people wanting to start a new business have to depend on banks or investors for the money they need.

   _____

   _____

3. High fuel costs made airline ticket prices rise even faster than they normally would have.

   _____

   _____

4. Slowly, over the course of several years, the company changed the way its products were packaged.

   _____

   _____

5. Our public relations department tried to improve our image, but negative stories in newspapers and on the Internet made their efforts ineffective.

   _____

   _____

6. Stricter government regulation is entirely the wrong approach.

   _____

   _____

7. Computerized manufacturing brought the company into an exciting new era.

   _____

   _____

8. If you try to skip some steps in the production process, the quality of your product will fall.

_____

_____

9. Because of mild weather this winter, our supplies were delivered on schedule, without the interruptions normally caused by snowstorms.

_____

_____

10. Government regulators began a program to monitor a huge number of pharmacies all across the nation.

_____

_____

MATCHING

Match each item in the left column with the best description from the right column.

1. charter flight _____

2. domestic flight _____

3. free market _____

4. labor union _____

5. net operating loss _____

6. nonstop flight _____

7. operating revenue _____

8. roundtrip flight _____

9. stiff opposition _____

a. money from business activity that is used to run the company

b. business expenses are greater than money earned

c. starts at one airport, goes to another, and then comes back

d. goes directly to its final destination

e. buyers and sellers come together without many restrictions

f. does not go from one country to another

g. an organization that represents workers in their dealings with managers

h. stands firmly against something

i. involves an airplane that is rented or leased

Reading Focus
Putting Reading to Work

WRITING

Do some research on ONE of these questions. Use one or two reference sources outside this chapter to gather information. You may use print or online resources. Write a short report (about 250 words) comparing the information you find in your research to the information in the reading.

Who benefits the most from strict government control over airline service?

Who benefits the most from free competition in the airline business?

Second Tier: Big Versus Small

Pre-Reading

DISCUSSION

This reading discusses the differences between large airlines and small airlines. Before you read, discuss the questions in a small group. Use a dictionary and other reference sources as necessary.

1. Do you prefer flying with a small airline or a legacy airline—a big airline with a major hub?

2. What are the advantages and disadvantages to each?

3. If you were an entrepreneur, what goal would you have for a new airline?

Reading

No Size Fits

1 In a way, the airline business puts everyone in an impossible situation. Small airlines wish they were big, but when they become big they wish they were small again. Every solution to an airline's problems seems to come at a huge sacrifice to the company, its stockholders, and the economy in general. But this almost insurmountable difficulty is some of what makes airlines interesting. This is why risk-loving entrepreneurs with a lot of money behind them start airlines instead of, say, automobile dealerships. The brash and talented founder of an airline brands his or her personal character not onto some docile cow but onto a charging rhino, a beast that may not make it to adulthood but enjoys a wild ride trying.

2 We speak of "small" airlines, but the term is decidedly relative. The huge expenditures necessary to get a company's first jet off the tarmac ensure that only well-funded players come to the table. A new Airbus A380 jet has a list price above $200 million. If this model, which can carry about 550 passengers, is too roomy, you can save considerably by opting for the 124-passenger A320, which costs a mere $60 million. No matter how an airline builds its fleet, the price tag for basic machinery is dizzying. Add other fixed costs like fuel, insurance, maintenance, and employee compensation, and even the smallest airline is spending more to operate than an average-sized cereal manufacturer.

3 In most businesses, an entrepreneur stunned by high startup costs could look forward to economies of scale. For example, a company that makes digital music equipment hopes to sell well enough to get very big, make millions of music players the size of business cards, and see the manufacturing cost of each player spread over these millions of units instead of over a paltry 300,000 or so. That is "scaling"—your costs per unit decrease as you achieve higher volume. In a scalable business, the cost of earning every additional dollar goes down. This may be dull, but it works. This is why businesses want to grow.

4 There is a real question as to whether airlines can ever be scalable. In a sense, an airline's product is the ticket, or, to be more precise, the "seat miles" that the ticket represents. A seat mile is a mile flown by a passenger. A flight that takes 50 passengers 500 miles generates 25,000 seat miles. For a single flight, you can see some scalability. If the flight takes 100 passengers 500 miles, it generates twice the seat miles it did with 50 on board. Since it costs essentially the same to fly the plane full as to fly it half-full, the airline benefits from economies of scale. Every new seat mile costs the airline less. Every new dollar it takes in on the flight costs less to generate.

5 The problem comes when you view the airline as a whole, not as the sum of its flights. The older an airline becomes, the more its costs rise. In other words, it does not benefit from economies of scale, which might be expected to bring the cost of each seat mile down as more seat miles are generated. Many factors work against the scalability of airlines, but the largest one by far is the cost of labor.

6 It takes highly skilled workers to fly a plane, perform maintenance on it, and ensure that passengers are safe and happy. Nothing about an airline's full-time workforce is cheap or short-term. This expensive band of specialists wants good pay, job security, and the other benefits that create stability. In the past, these elements of the good life were protected by labor unions, which negotiated healthy contracts for their members. As we'll see later in our discussion of legacy airlines, these contracts turned into enormous millstones around a company's neck as its employees aged and retired. Newer, smaller airlines still need a stable, happy crew of highly skilled specialists, but they have to achieve this without mediating their employer-employee relations through an old-style union contract.

7 This can be done. The great success story of JetBlue illustrates how a small airline can do it. Through the personal charisma of a brilliant entrepreneur with a people-oriented approach, a highly skilled group of employees can be made to feel like a team that gets along just fine with the coach. But a change in the coaching staff, or the expansion of the team so the head coach sees each player once a year if at all, can disrupt this harmony. Labor unrest, mass resignations, interrupted schedules and loss

of public trust may all result. In other words, each step toward bigness actually costs the airline more instead of leading to economies of scale. As the old adage goes, if you have to be Superman to run it, it isn't scalable.

8 At the other end of the spectrum are the "legacy" airlines, the big operations that use a hub-and-spoke system and have been around since before airline deregulation in 1978. Their problem is baggage, decades of encumbrances from expensive labor contracts, investments in too much equipment, overinvestment in hub facilities, and organizational structures that creak under their own weight. It is not even worth describing all the employee-compensation problems of a typical legacy airline. Suffice it to say its old union contracts force it to pay pensions and the costs of health insurance for tens of thousands of people who don't even work there anymore. And that says nothing about their obligations to current employees.

9 Troubles for the mega-airlines routinely spill over into the communities they serve. The case of Northwest Airlines is a perfect example. Based in Minneapolis-St. Paul, Northwest alienated the public in its own home state in the 1990s by demanding, and receiving, money from the state of Minnesota and the city of Duluth for the construction of a maintenance facility near the Duluth airport in northern Minnesota. Northwest ultimately brought far fewer than the predicted number of jobs to the area and then closed the facility in 2005. The airline had threatened in the early 1990s to file for bankruptcy unless Minnesota gave it more than $800 million in low-cost loans. The loss of Northwest's contribution to Minnesota's economy was a horrifying prospect to public officials. Minnesota came through with the money, but the wisdom of the aid came into question. The deal looked even worse when Northwest declared bankruptcy in late 2005, a status that exempted it (at least temporarily) from paying its debts.

10 With Northwest's 2005 declaration, fully two-thirds of the legacy airlines in the United States were technically bankrupt. This represented a strategic use of legal resources in order to avoid problems and gain advantages. Bankruptcy does not ground an airline. Northwest, Delta, and other bankrupt airlines continued to fly schedules nearly the same as their pre-filing grids. The difference is that the bankruptcy court may relieve them of obligations to their workers, their suppliers, and even their investors if the court thinks these obligations pose too great a burden. Obviously, such freedom from normal business obligations gives a bankrupt airline a huge advantage over non-bankrupt competitors, especially those from other countries. Since the most profitable routes for many big U.S. airlines bring them into competition with Singapore Airlines, British Air, Alitalia, Swissair, and others, an advantage over foreign competitors can mean a lot of money.

11 But it's not much of a way to go through life—shedding your debts, declaring yourself a financial failure (which many bankrupt airlines are

not, actually), destroying any trust that might exist between you and your creditors. Bankruptcy is also far better for lawyers than for anyone else in the process. To say that big airlines want to be bankrupt is to assume no love of the industry among the company's top executives.

12 In the end, this love of the plane and its possibilities is what keeps many executives coming back for more. Each hopes to be tremendously lucky, to dodge obstacles beyond industry control such as terrorist attacks, government regulations, fuel shortages, or economic recessions. Each hopes to be the one to overcome some technical challenge, to champion a new relationship between management and employees, to invent the perfect route structure, to achieve scalability with growth, or to steer an old airline out of the fog of the past. Each hopes to show that there's no discontinuity between the small and the large, and that the large no longer need beach themselves.

Post-Reading

Basic Comprehension

MULTIPLE CHOICE

Circle the choice that best answers each question.

1. Which of the following best states the main idea of Paragraph 2?
   a. Even 60 million is a lot of money.
   b. Even getting a jet off the tarmac is expensive.
   c. Even large airlines can be considered "small."
   d. Even "small" airlines are expensive to operate.

2. According to the reading, individual flights can achieve economies of scale because
   a. as the number of passengers rises, so does the number of seat miles
   b. as the number of passengers rises, the cost of each new seat mile drops
   c. as the number of seat miles rises, so does the cost of operating the flight
   d. as the number of seat miles rises, the number of passengers drops

3. In what way do labor costs make it difficult for airlines to achieve scalability?

    a. Labor costs go up as an airline grows.

    b. Labor unions do not like to negotiate with large airlines.

    c. Large airlines' workforces are cheap and short-term.

    d. Large airlines must hire older workers.

Reading Focus

Integrating Information

PREDICTING

The reading in Tier 2 weaves in many subtopics and expresses views about several aspects of the airline business. Some of these are substantial enough to be possible topics for a writing assignment. Others are not. List six subtopics from the reading that you think might be possible writing topics.

_____

_____

_____

_____

_____

_____

INTERPRETING

You must be able to recognize exactly what a writing assignment asks for.

A. Read the writing assignment and the explanation of what it is asking for. Make a list of what you would include in any response to this prompt.

> In one or two paragraphs (about 100–200 words), explain why the title of this reading, "No Size Fits," appropriately describes the airline industry. Use information from the reading in your response. You may also use information from the other readings in this unit, if you like. Use your own words.

B. Compare your list with this list. A good response must have these features.

- *In one or two paragraphs (about 100–200 words)* . . . The assignment calls for a very short piece of writing. The teacher giving such an assignment does not expect a long essay.
- *. . . explain why the title of this reading, "No Size Fits," appropriately describes the airline industry.* This is the heart of the assignment. It asks for an explanation—not a physical description, not persuasion, not narration (a story), and not a personal opinion. This explanation must focus on the relationship between the short title and the airlines: why is there apparently no good size for an airline?
- *Use information from the reading in your response. You may also use information from the other readings in this unit, if you like.* This lists acceptable sources for any information you may include in your writing. You must use information from the reading. You may—but are not required to—use the other readings in this unit for ideas as well. The teacher is looking for information that can be judged as true or false based on what this unit says. Do not waste time or space on information from your personal experience or from what you may have learned through other sources.

- *Use your own words.* The teacher will give a low score to a piece of writing that copies substantial phrases from the reading(s). A goal of the assignment is to assess your English-language writing, not the words of the original authors. The "don't copy" rule usually applies to strings of three or more words. Some very basic vocabulary items (e.g, *have, make, cause*) can be borrowed without the appearance of copying. So can specialized terms that cannot easily be rephrased in common English (e.g., *scalability, airline industry, file for bankruptcy*). However, a phrase like *ensure that passengers are safe and happy* should not be borrowed. It is more than three words long and is distinctive. It is clearly in the voice of the original author. It could be rephrased in several ways. If you decide to use this idea, you have to call on your English vocabulary to paraphrase it in words of your own.

MULTIPLE CHOICE

Read this writing assignment. Circle the item that best describes what the assignment asks for.

> According to the readings in this unit, airlines have to manage substantial costs. In an essay of four or five paragraphs, outline some of these costs and the efforts that have been made to control them. Use information from any of the readings in this unit. Use your own words.

1. About how long should the essay for this assignment be?
   a. 200–300 words
   b. 600–800 words
   c. 1,200–1,500 words
   d. 2,000–2,500 words

2. What should the essay mainly accomplish?
   a. name several airline costs and show how they might be limited
   b. compare the cost-control efforts of airlines with those of other businesses
   c. explain the factors that make airline costs difficult to control
   d. show how several actual airlines have managed their costs

3. What information must the essay contain?

   a. facts from the reading

   b. personal experience

   c. details from unit

   d. all of the above

4. This assignment tells you to use your own words. Which phrase from the reading should NOT be used in an essay for this assignment.

   a. for example

   b. every seat mile

   c. labor union

   d. declaring yourself a financial failure

Putting Reading to Work

WRITING

The following writing assignments ask you to use information from this unit. Your teacher may require you to do one or more of the following assignments to show what you have learned from the readings and if you can integrate information from outside resources.

1. In one or two paragraphs (about 100–200) words, explain why both large and small airlines seem to have problems. Use information from "No Size Fits" in your response. You may also use information from the other readings in this unit, if you like. Use your own words.

2. According to the readings in this unit, the hub-and-spoke system has advantages and disadvantages. In an essay of four or five paragraphs, argue either that the disadvantages outweigh the advantages or vice versa. Use information from any of the readings in this unit to support your argument. Use your own words.

3. In 1978, legislation was passed that deregulated the airlines. In an essay of four or five paragraphs, outline the pros and cons of this act and how you think it affected the state of the airlines today. Use information from any of the readings in this unit or consult one or two outside references. Use your own words.

Third Tier: Scalability

Pre-Reading

DISCUSSION

Air travel in the United States has generally increased since the 1970s (except for a few short interruptions due to economic recession or fear of terrorism). The ever-greater number of airline passengers is still routed through several major hub airports around the country. Some major airports handle so many flights now that they have no room for any more. They cannot increase revenue by adding any more flights, and congestion at the airports contributes to ever-increasing delays and discomfort for passengers. This reading discusses these issues. Before you read, discuss the questions in a small group.

1. What are some ways of solving airport congestion problems? Consider potential actions by these entities:

   Individual private airlines: _____

   Individual airports: _____

   Regions served by hubs: _____

   The federal government: _____

2. After developing a list of potential solutions, devise a plan to implement the best solution. Present your solution to the class.

Reading

Scalability and Evolutionary Dynamics
of Air Transportation Networks
in the United States

Abstract

1 With the growing demand for air transportation and the limited ability to increase capacity at key points in the air transportation system, there are concerns that, in the future, the system will not scale to meet demand. This situation will result in the generation and the propagation of delays throughout the system, impacting passengers' quality of travel, and more broadly, the economy. There is, therefore, the need to investigate the mechanisms by which the air transportation system scaled to meet demand in the past and will do so in the future. In order to investigate limits to scale of current air transportation networks, theories of scale-free and scalable networks were used. It was found that the U.S. air transportation network is not scalable at the airport level due to capacity constraints. However, the results of a case study analysis of multi-airport systems that led to the aggregation of these multiple airports into single nodes and the analysis of this network showed that the air transportation network was scalable at the regional level. In order to understand how the network evolves, an analysis of the scaling dynamics that influence the structure of the network was conducted. Initially, the air transportation network scales according to airport-level mechanisms—through the addition of capacity and the improvement of efficiency—but as infrastructure constraints are reached, higher-level scaling mechanisms such as the emergence of secondary airports and the construction of new high-capacity airports are triggered. These findings suggest that, given current and future limitations on the ability to add capacity at certain airports, regional-level scaling mechanisms will be key to accommodating future needs for air transportation.

I. Introduction

2 With the growing demand for air transportation and the limited ability to increase capacity at key points in the air transportation system there are concerns that, in the future, the system will not scale to meet demand. Historically, air traffic has grown significantly. Revenue passenger kilometers [RPK] have increased by a factor of 3.3 from 393 billion in 1978 to 1.304 billion in 2005 [1]. Assuming a similar rate of growth to the rate of growth that

prevailed between 1985 and 2005, passenger traffic would approach 1.9 billion RPKs by 2025. Several forecasts also indicate significant growth of traffic in the next decades [2][3][4][5]. However, infrastructure capacity constraints at airports create congestion that results in aircraft and passenger delays that propagate throughout the system. In the 1990s, passenger and aircraft traffic increased and reached a peak in 2000.

3 Concurrently, delays increased to reach a peak in 2000. While there was a generalized stress over the system due to traffic loads, a localized capacity crisis at La Guardia airport created record high delays. As a result of the slowdown of the economy and Sept. 11 events, passenger and aircraft traffic decreased in 2001, which relieved pressure on the system thus decreasing delays. Starting in 2003 with a localized capacity crisis at Chicago O'Hare airport and with later a general increase in number of operations, delays increased again to reach a record high of 22.1 million minutes of delays in 2006. Projections of delays for 2007 indicated that a new record was likely to be set. The generation of delays and their propagation throughout the system negatively impact air transportation quality of service, passengers' quality of travel, and the economy.

4 Given the growing demand for air transportation in the future and inherent key capacity constraints, there are concerns that,

in the future, the system will not scale to meet demand. This motivates the need to investigate the mechanisms by which the air transportation system scaled to meet demand in the past and will do so in the future.

II. *Methodology and Data Used for the Network Analysis*

5 Because the air transportation system is fundamentally a network system (composed of thousands of interconnected subsystems and parts), it can be described and represented using network abstractions and tools from network theory. In addition, recent theories of scale-free and scalable networks were used as a starting point for the analysis [6] [7] [8] [9] [10] [11]. The network of interest for this research is the flight/aircraft flow network for which the nodes are airports and the arcs are non-stop origin-destination routes. In order to analyze the structure of the current U.S. air transport network, a cross-sectional analysis was performed using actual aircraft-traffic data from the Federal Aviation Administration's (FAA) Enhanced Traffic Management System (ETMS) [12]. For each flight, this database provided the aircraft type, the airports of departure and arrival, the aircraft position (latitude, longitude and altitude), and speed information.

6 For the extraction of the network structural information, data

of 365 days of traffic was analyzed (from October 1st 2004 to September 30th 2005). In addition to the detailed ETMS flight database, a library of civil airplanes corresponding to 869 ETMS aircraft codes was used. The ETMS airport database was crossed with the FAA Form 5010 airport database [13] that provided additional airport information such as runway characteristics (i.e. length, pavement type). In the following analysis 12,007 public and private airports—of any runway length—were used for the extraction of flights from the ETMS flight database. An extensive data quality assurance process was used to filter data with missing information fields such as aircraft type and clearly flawed trajectory data. In addition, international flights and military and helicopter operations were filtered out. The retained data accounted for 70 percent of the total number of flights from the original data. The data was also filtered into categories of aircraft (in order to understand the differences in terms of network structure between various modes of operations). These categories included; widebody jets (e.g. Boeing 767, Airbus 300), narrow-body jets (e.g. Boeing 737s, Airbus 318/319/320/321), regional jets (e.g. Bombardier CRJ200, Embraer E145), business jets (e.g. Cessna CJ1, Hawker 400), turboprops (e.g. Q400, ATR42), and piston aircraft (e.g. Cessna 172, Pipers). From this detailed flight data, network adjacency matrices were constructed for each of the aircraft types.

> Note: The authors of this reading treat *data* as a singular, non-count noun, e.g. "The data was also filtered . . . " Many other writers treat *data* as a plural noun (singular *datum*), e.g. "The data were collected . . . "

7 The ETMS traffic data showed that the frequency of flights on each U.S. flight route (ranging from 1 to 1,000 flights per year) varied according to the kind of aircraft being flown. The wide-body jet network is primarily composed of relatively few long-haul cross-country flights, most of which operate with fairly high frequency. The narrow-body jet network is denser, with relatively shorter range flights and some routes with very high frequency (i.e., over 900 flights per month or 30 flights per day). The network of flights flown by regional jets is sparse, with high-frequency routes mainly centered on hubs such as Chicago O'Hare (ORD), Atlanta (ATL), Denver (DEN), etc. which is consistent with the dominant use of the regional jets as feeders to hub operations.

8 While the wide-body, narrow-body, and regional jet networks are relatively sparse, the networks of flights flown by business jets, turboprops, and light piston aircraft

are denser. The business-jet network is dense with low-frequency routes. However, there are a few popular (i.e. medium-frequency) routes between key metropolitan regions such as New York, Chicago, Dallas, Atlanta, Miami, Denver, Los Angeles, etc. The turboprop network exhibits both a dense set of low-frequency routes and a localized set of routes that are centered on key airports. This latter part of the network is formed by feeder flights in and out of connecting hub airports. Finally, the piston-aircraft network, which is the network that spans across the largest number of airports, is composed mainly of low-frequency routes. This is consistent with the type of use and unscheduled operations performed by light piston aircraft.

III. Analysis of the U.S. Air Transportation Network at the Airport Level

9 The U.S. air transportation network is a woven set of networks or layers (networks composed of airports—nodes and origin destination routes, which can be thought of as lines or arcs between nodes). In combination, these layers form the overall U.S. air transportation network. This overall network is composed of a large set of low-frequency routes and a more limited set of very-high-frequency routes. Despite the large number of nodes present in this network, aircraft traffic is concentrated at only a few key airports. In fact, 30 airports handle

almost 80 percent of the overall traffic. One of the key metrics that characterizes the structure of a network is the degree distribution. The degree of a node is the number of incoming and outgoing arcs to and from this node (i.e. number of routes connecting one airport to other airports in the network). A large number of nodes (i.e. airports) exhibit low numbers of destinations (i.e. node degree) while there are very few airports that have large numbers of destinations.

10 While the degree of a node captures information regarding the number of destinations to and from an airport, it does not capture any information regarding the frequency of flights on the arcs and ultimately the number of flights at each airport. The degree of a node can be weighted by the number of flights on incoming and outgoing arcs which is referred to as a flight weighted degree.

IV. Analysis of the U.S. Air Transportation Network at the Regional Level

11 Because of the trend of emergence of secondary airports in the vicinity of primary airports, leading to the development of multi-airport systems, additional insight can be gained by examining the system at the regional level [14]. A regional airport system was defined as all airports within 50 miles of one of the identified airports. For the purpose of this analysis, a primary airport was defined as an airport

serving between 20 percent and 100 percent of the passenger traffic in the region and secondary airports were defined as serving between one percent and 20 percent of the traffic. Other airports serving less than one percent of the traffic in the region were not considered for further detailed analysis.

12 Let us consider two cases of regional airport systems in which multiple airports serving more than one percent of the passenger traffic were found. The Boston region, which is centered around Boston Logan (BOS) airport, features two other significant airports: Manchester (MHT) airport in New Hampshire and Providence (PVD) airport in Rhode Island. While Boston Logan is considered a primary airport, Manchester and Providence airports are considered to be secondary airports. While Boston is an example of a single-primary-airport system, there are more complex multi-airport systems with multiple primary airports and secondary airports such as the New York region. The New York airport system has three primary airports: New York La Guardia (LGA), John F. Kennedy (JFK) and Newark (ERW). In addition, the region also has a secondary airport located on Long Island—Islip McArthur airport (ISP). A total of 16 primary and 16 secondary airports were found in the 11 multi-airport systems in the United States. The remaining 15 of the top 29 airports are single-primary-airport systems.

13 From a network perspective, the emergence of a new primary and secondary airport implies new connections to the rest of the network of airports. For example, the emergence of Providence airport as part of the Boston regional airport system has led to the creation of origin-destination (OD) pairs such as PVD-ORD (a secondary to primary airport market) and PVD-MDW (a secondary to secondary airport market). These routes are parallel to the primary-to-primary airport route— BOS-ORD. Using Form 41 traffic data for the months of March 1990 and 2003, capturing respectively a total of 18,000 and 15,000 distinct OD pairs, the number of OD pairs for each category was computed for both periods [15].

14 It was found that semi-parallel networks (i.e. primary-to-secondary airport network) grew by 13 percent in terms of number of routes served between 1990 and 2003. The largest growth was observed in the parallel network category (i.e. secondary-to-secondary airport network) where a 49 percent growth occurred between 1990 and 2003. This phenomenon is mainly due to the emergence and growth of secondary airports in the 1990s (e.g. Providence, Manchester, etc). The introduction of new OD pairs between one secondary airport and another is the result of the strategy of carriers like Southwest that operate largely at secondary airports and connect them together with point-to-point flights.

15 Because the primary and secondary airports that were identified in each of the regional airport systems serve the demand for air transportation within the same region, these airports can be aggregated into one multi-airport system node. A new network composed of the 11 multi-airport nodes and the 2,159 single-airport nodes was constructed. Similarly to the single airport node network, the flight weighted degree distribution of this new network was examined. This led to a finding that the mechanisms by which new airports emerged in a region are key to the ability of the system to scale and to meet demand.

Note: The reading includes some technical terms from statistics. Some of these, such as *preferential attachment dynamic*, are partially explained. Others, such as *power law distribution*, are not. You do not need to understand these terms to get the main ideas in the reading. Develop the ability to see beyond technical vocabulary to larger meanings.

V. Historical Evolution of Nodes in the U.S. Air Transportation Network

16 The presence of a power law distribution implies that there exists an underlying growth mechanism based on preferential attachment [6][9][10]. This preferential attachment dynamic implies that a node grows proportionally to its size in the network (in an unconstrained case). From an air transportation system perspective, the preferential attachment mechanism implies that new flights added to the network are added to airports proportionally to the size of these airports in the network. Airports that already have a significant number of flights are more likely to attract flights than airports with no traffic. This is consistent with network-planning behaviors that are generally observed in the air transportation industry where airlines have incentives to add flights to an airport that they are already serving rather than another closely located non-utilized airport.

17 Using historical data from the FAA Terminal Area Forecast database that covers the time period from 1976 to 2005, an analysis of the historical growth rate of airports was performed [5]. It was found that the average growth rate versus weight of the node in terms of traffic deviates from a hypothetical linear relation for individual airports (Figure 1).

18 If the nodes had aligned with the hypothetical line, this would have indicated preferential attachment growth. The observed deviation is not surprising and was expected due to capacity constraints that limit the growth of certain airports (e.g. Washington National (DCA), John F. Kennedy (JFK), New York La Guardia (LGA),

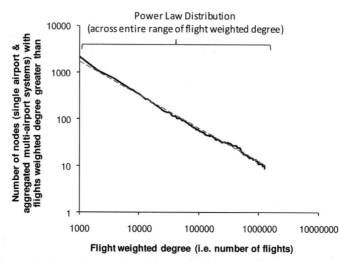

Figure 1: Flight weighted degree distribution of the network with aggregated multi-airport.

and Chicago O'Hare (ORD). In fact, four out of the 29 airports are constrained by capacity through the use of slot restrictions. Other airports such as Newark (EWR), Atlanta (ATL), Boston (BOS), and San Francisco (SFO) exhibit delays that are signs of demand/capacity inadequacy. Airports above the hypothetical linear growth line—those exhibiting super linear growth—such as Cincinnati (CVG), Washington Dulles (IAD), [and] Dallas Fort Worth (DFW)—are airports that grew significantly because they became hubs in the time horizon of the analysis. The analysis was also extended to the average growth rate of regional airport systems (Figure 2).

19 This relationship—average growth rate versus traffic share—was also analyzed for two types of nodes: multi-airport and single-airport. It was found that for multi-airport system nodes, the deviations from the linear relationship are significantly reduced, which implies that preferential attachment dynamics govern the nodes of the network at the regional level. There are, however, some deviations from the linear relationship that can be explained by differences in regional economic growth (i.e. South West vs. North East) for the higher-than-linear growth rates (i.e. super-linear growth). In addition, it is believed that the lower growth rate of New York multi-airport system node is due in part to regional level constraints such as airspace capacity limits.

VI. Scaling Dynamics in the U.S. Air Transportation System

20 A detailed analysis of the 15 single airport systems and 11 multi-airport systems (covering 48

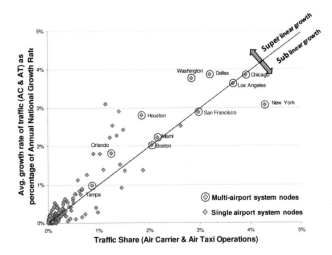

Figure 2: Average rate of growth of single and multi-airport system nodes vs. traffic share in the network (from 1976 to 2005).

airports in the United States) led to the identification of key scaling dynamics by which the air transportation system scales to meet demand. It was found that latent demand for air transportation materializes into passenger traffic in the presence of a supply of air transportation services (i.e. air transportation networks). This supply of air transportation services is supported by an underlying infrastructure formed by the national airport system. From a system-performance standpoint, limited capacity at airports and high demand lead to a demand/capacity inadequacy problem. This problem manifests itself in general with the generation of delays and their propagation throughout the network. As delays increase and negative impacts on quality of travel

arise, pressure to solve the problem grows. Several solutions are available to address this problem. One possible response, the "do nothing" option, assumes a self-regulating mechanism (i.e. delay homeostasis) based on a level of delays that airlines and passengers are willing to bear. Another set of solutions is to implement demand-management schemes whether they are regulatory based mechanisms or market-based mechanisms. However none of these solutions increases the capacity of the system. Rather, each attempts to address the problem by limiting demand and growth of traffic. A set of solutions that allow the system to scale and meet demand incorporates scaling dynamics.

21 There are three classes of fundamental scaling dynamics.

- **Traffic shift mechanisms**

Traffic shift mechanisms can involve both temporal and spatial shifts. The temporal utilization of an airport throughout a day is highly variable due to temporal demand patterns (i.e. early mornings and late afternoons are high peak demand periods and middle of the day and nights are low demand periods of activity), but is also due to airline scheduling behaviors. Airlines operate connecting hub airports with a succession of banks of arrivals and departures roughly every hour. While it is difficult to smooth passenger demand uniformly across the day and night because of passenger traveling constraints and preferences, over the last 5 years airlines have been active at debanking the operations at connecting hub airports by smoothing the operations (i.e. implementation of the rolling hub concept).

22 While the previous mechanisms focused on temporal shifts of traffic, traffic can also be shifted spatially with regional based scaling mechanisms (i.e. scaling "out" to existing nodes) involving the emergence of secondary airports. Over the last three decades, several key secondary airports have emerged in the United States serving demand for air transportation within a region. While passengers who live in secondary basins of population within a metropolitan region (e.g. Manchester in New Hampshire, Providence in Rhode Island) used to travel to the single primary airport serving a region, with the emergence of new airports serving the region they can fly directly from a closer and less congested airport.

- **Efficiency improvements and procedural changes**

23 Another set of scaling dynamics involves local efficiency improvements. From a network perspective, efficiency can be improved at the nodes (i.e. airports) with mechanisms such as runway-efficiency improvements, reduction of separation of aircraft on approach, and better utilization of multi-runway operation through greater optimization of sequencing, etc. In addition, efficiency can be improved at the arc level (i.e. flight/route level) by increasing the average size of aircraft (i.e. scaling "up" arcs). From a transportation-system-performance perspective, the true metric of efficiency is the number of passengers carried by unit of capacity. Therefore, utilizing larger aircraft increases the passenger throughput while using the same airport resources. However, the increased competition in the airline industry in the post-deregulation era, and the race for higher flight frequency, has driven the decrease in average aircraft size. In fact, in the last 16 years, the average size of aircraft in the United States— for domestic operations—has decreased from 130 to 88 seats. One

of the key phenomena underlying this trend was the entry and use of 50-to 90-seat Regional Jets (RJs) in the 1990s. The use of these aircraft is substantial at major airports such as Chicago O'Hare (ORD) and La Guardia (LGA) for which the traffic share of regional jets was 43 percent and 32 percent respectively, in 2005.

- **Physical capacity enhancement mechanisms**

24 Finally, the system can scale by the addition of physical capacity. Both local airport and regional airport system based mechanisms can lead to an increase in physical capacity of infrastructure serving a region. The airport-level-based mechanism involves the construction of new runways if this is feasible. The incremental gain in capacity resulting from the construction of a new runway can be highly variable. For example, the new 14/32 runway at Boston Logan airport that entered into service in 2006 after a 30-year planning process is only generating a capacity benefit of approximately three percent due to low annual utilization because of its use in certain rare wind conditions. On the other hand, new runways such as the new runway at Atlanta Hartsfield airport will lead to a 33 percent capacity increase. Another physical-capacity-enhancement mechanism (i.e. scaling "out" to new nodes) involves the construction of new large-capacity airports in the

region. This regional-level-based mechanism was observed in the United States in the 1970s with the construction of airports such as Washington Dulles (IAD), Dallas Fort Worth (DFW) and more recently with Denver International (DEN) in the 1990s. Due to strong environmental constraints, it is increasingly hard to build new large- capacity airports and even runways at key airports. In addition, the gains in capacity due to efficiency improvements such as runway utilization optimization and remaining debanking opportunities are limited and can only provide marginal capacity improvements on the order of a few percentage points. Given the existence of a dense network of underutilized airports in the United States, the scaling mechanism involving the emergence of secondary airports, using existing underutilized infrastructure, is seen as a key mechanism for scaling the air transportation network and system and meeting future demand.

VII. *Conclusions*

25 From the analysis of the air transportation network structure and the detailed analysis of regional airport systems, it was found that the U.S. air transportation network is not scalable at the airport level due to capacity constraints. However, the analysis of the U.S. air transportation network for which multiple airports serving a region were aggregated into one multiairport system node based on the

analysis of case studies of regional airports systems showed that the network is scale-free and scalable. In order to understand how the network evolves, an analysis of the scaling mechanisms and the factors that influence the structure of the network was performed. Initially, the air transportation network scaled according to airport level mechanisms—through the addition of capacity and the improvement in efficiency. In the absence of constraints, the air transportation network scales according to the preferential attachment scaling mechanisms. However, as infrastructure constraints are reached, higher-level scaling mechanisms, such as the emergence of secondary airports and the construction of new high-capacity airports, are triggered.

26 Given the fact that there is a limited capability for adding capacity at major airports, these findings suggest that regional-level scaling mechanisms will be key to accommodating future needs for air transportation. The attractiveness of existing underutilized airports will increase leading to the growth of existing secondary airports and the emergence of new secondary airports.

Acknowledgments

27 This work was supported by NASA Langley under grant NAG-1-2038 and by the FAA under contract DTFA01-01-C-00030'D.0#16. The authors would like to thank Professor Alexandre Bayen from Berkeley University for his help with accessing ETMS data. In addition, the authors thank the NASA/FAA Joint University Program participants for their feedback.

Biographies

28 **Philippe A. Bonnefoy** is a Ph.D. candidate in the Engineering Systems Division (ESD) at MIT and he is conducting research at the MIT International Center for Air Transportation. He holds a Master of Science in Aeronautics and Astronautics from MIT and a Bachelor of Science in Aerospace Engineering from Ecole Polytechnique de Montreal in Canada. His current research focuses on the investigation of the scalability of air transportation networks and the evaluation of the implications of changes in the use of the airport infrastructure on the air transportation system. He also works on modeling and simulating Very Light Jet based air taxi networks and the integration of these new vehicles in the National Air Transportation System.

29 **R. John Hansman** has been on the faculty of the Department of Aeronautics and Astronautics at MIT since 1982. He obtained his A.B. in Physics from Cornell University in 1976, his S.M. in Physics in 1980 and his Ph.D. in Physics, Meteorology, Aeronautics and Astronautics, and Electrical Engineering from MIT in 1982. He is the Director of the MIT International Center for Air Transportation. His current research

activities focus on advanced information systems and complex system issues in the operational domains of air traffic control, airline operations, and aircraft cockpits.

References

[1] Annual Review of Civil Aviation, 2005, published in *ICAO Journal*.

[2] Federal Aviation Administration. *Aerospace Forecasts 2005–2016*. FAA, 2005.

[3] Federal Aviation Administration, *Aerospace Forecasts 2005–2016*, available at: http://www.api.faa.gov/forecast05/Forecast_for_2005.htm

[4] Joint Planning and Development Office. "Next Generation of Air Transportation System Progress Report 2005." Washington, 2005.

[5] Terminal Area Forecast Historical Data, available at: http://www.apo.data.faa.gov/main/taf.asp, 2006.

[6] Newman M. E. J., "The structure and function of complex networks." Society for Industrial and Applied Mathematics, p.167–256, 2003.

[7] Dorogovstev S.N., Mendes J.F.F., "Evolution of networks," Oxford University Press, 2003.

[8] Guimera R., Mossa S., Turschi A., Nunes Amaral L., 2004, "Structure and Efficiency of the World-Wide Airport Network," arXiv:cond-mat/0312535 v1 19 Dec 2003.

[9] Krapivsky P.L., and Redner S., "Organization of growing random networks," *Physical Review E*, Volume 63, 066123, 2001, pp.1–14.

[10] Li L., Alderson D., Doyle J., Willinger W. "Towards a Theory of Scale-Free Graphs: Definition, Properties, and Implications." *Internet Mathematics*. Vol. 2m, No. 4, 2005: pp. 431–523.

[11] Barrat A., Barthelemy M., Vespignani A., "The effects of spatial constraints on networks," *J. Stat. Mech.* P05003, 2005.

[12] Enhanced Traffic Management System (ETMS), Data from Sept 30, 2004 to Oct 1, 2005.

[13] United States Department of Transportation Federal Aviation Administration, Form 5010 data, available at: http://www.gcr1.com/5010web, Last accessed: July 2004.

[14] Bonnefoy P., Hansman R. J., "Emergence of Secondary Airports and Dynamics of Multi-airport Systems," Master Thesis Massachusetts Institute of Technology, 2005.

[15] Bureau of Transportation Statistics, Aviation, Airline Origin and Destination Survey DB1B, available at: http://www.transtats.bts.gov/, last accessed: December 2004.

Post-Reading

Basic Comprehension

SHORT ANSWER

Answer the questions briefly (1–3 sentences) in your own words.

1. What problem does this paper address?

    _____

    _____

2. What is "scalability"?

    _____

    _____

3. What would result from the air transportation system's being unable to continue to scale to meet rising demand?

    _____

    _____

4. According to the paper's conclusions, how can the air transportation continue to scale in the future?

    _____

    _____

MULTIPLE CHOICE

Circle the choice that answers each question.

1. Between 2001 and 2003, what occurred as a result of the September 11 terrorist attacks?

   a. A decrease in passenger numbers resulted in fewer flight delays.
   b. Government regulation kept the number of flight delays low.
   c. Increased security led to longer flight delays.
   d. Reduced aircraft traffic led to more flight delays.

2. Which statements best describe the authors' findings regarding the U.S. air-transportation network at the airport level? (Choose two.)

   a. There are very few airports that offer only a very limited number of flights and routes.
   b. There are very few airports that offer a large number of flights and routes.
   c. There are many airports that offer only a very limited number of flights and routes.
   d. There are many airports that offer a large number of flights and routes.

3. What can be most strongly inferred from paragraphs 11–15 about New York La Guardia (LGA), John F. Kennedy (JFK), and Newark (ERW) airports?

   a. Each of them serves at least 20 percent of New York's passengers.
   b. One of them is a primary airport and the other two are secondary airports.
   c. Passengers prefer Islip McArthur airport (ISP) to them.
   d. They are all losing passengers and flights.

4. Which statement best states something the authors learned by using Form 41 traffic data?

   a. "It was found that semi-parallel networks (i.e. primary-to-secondary airport network) grew by 13 percent in terms of number of routes served."

   b. ". . . the emergence of Providence airport as part of the Boston regional airport system has led to the creation of origin-destination (OD) pairs . . ."

   c. "Using Form 41 traffic data for the month of March 1990 and 2003, . . . the number of OD pairs for each category was computed for both periods."

   d. "PVD-ORD (a secondary-to-primary airport market) and PVD-MDW (a secondary-to-secondary airport market) . . . are parallel to the primary to primary airport route—BOS-ORD."

5. Which of the following should be true if the "preferential attachment dynamic" is operating in the air transportation system?

   a. More new flights will be added to the airports with the fewest delays.

   b. More new flights will be awarded to the least crowded airports.

   c. Medium-sized airports will attract more flights than large or small airports.

   d. The more flights an airport has, the more new flights it will attract.

6. What reason is presented to partially explain why the New York airport system deviates from the linear relationship mentioned in Paragraphs 18 and 19.

   a. Economic growth has slowed down in the New York region.

   b. Competition from other nearby airport systems attracts flights away from New York.

   c. The airspace around New York already serves nearly as many flights as it can.

   d. Preferential attachment dynamics govern the New York system.

7. Which statement best describes the impact on the air-traffic system of following the "do nothing" approach?

   a. If nothing is done, airports will deteriorate so badly that the system will break down.

   b. If nothing is done, airlines will decide on their own to set up many new routes.

   c. If nothing is done, delays will increase so much that the system will break down.

   d. If nothing is done, delays will be common but passengers will tolerate them.

8. The reading suggests that all of the following can increase air traffic capacity EXCEPT

   a. temporal shifts

   b. demand management schemes

   c. spatial shifts to existing nodes

   d. runway efficiency improvements

9. The text suggests that the demand for smaller airplanes increased because _____.

   a. airlines competed to have more frequent flights

   b. smaller runways were constructed at many airports

   c. airlines had difficulty filling the seats of larger planes

   d. larger planes became too expensive to buy

10. Which of the proposed means of increasing air traffic capacity do the authors find most promising?

   a. Using existing little-used airports as secondary airports in regional systems.

   b. Building new large-capacity airports in regions that have reached their limits.

   c. Improving local efficiency in existing airports.

   d. Implementing market based mechanisms to manage demand.

Vocabulary

FILL IN THE BLANK

In each blank, write the best item from the list. Use each item only once. To correctly fill many blanks, the form of an item must be changed to fit the grammar of the sentence.

arc	dense	node	sparse
constraint	extract	propagate	spatial
degree	manifest	scale	temporal

1. Singapore is one of the most _____ populated nations in the world, with nearly 7,000 people per square kilometer.

2. During the 1990s, a capitalist approach to economics was widely adopted, even in countries that were nominally communist or socialist. As capitalism _____ throughout the world, opposition to it also increased, notably in South America.

3. British influence in former colonies remains. It _____ itself in many ways. For one, English remains an official or commercially dominant language in countries from Guyana, to Nigeria, to Malaysia.

4. In rural areas, a market town is vitally important to people's subsistence. It serves as a commercial _____, a center on which farmers and tradespeople converge from all directions. If we graphed travel in the region, we would see countless lines leading from farms and small villages to a busy central point—the market town.

5. The article was organized _____, discussing airline regulation from early in the 20th century, through the 1970s and 1980s, and on to the present day.

6. In many companies that provide Internet service, the management structure cannot _____ to meet the demands of success. It works well when the company is small, but it fails once the company has grown beyond a certain point.

7. We had a lot of information about our competitors. The challenge was for us to _____ some meaning from the data, some clues that could give us some advantage over them.

8. Think of each airport as a dot, or a node in the network. Any airline flight can be represented as a(n) _____ connecting two nodes. This model of lines and dots presents a picture of the network.

9. The coast of Namibia, in southern Africa, is one of the driest places on Earth. Trees are almost non-existent, and sources of groundwater are _____.

10. Many countries have wanted to expand but have faced _____ on the amount of available land within their borders. Some, such as the Netherlands and the United Arab Emirates, have responded by creating new land from areas previously covered by the sea.

11. Let's rank our spending priorities. Those with the greatest _____ of importance to our operations should get the most attention.

12. Cities in the Midwestern United States often spread out over vast areas of land because they faced almost no _____ constraints. There was always plenty of flat land to build on.

MULTIPLE CHOICE

Choose the word or phrase closest in meaning to the italicized word(s) in each sentence from the reading.

1. "These findings suggest that, given current and future limitations on the ability to add capacity at certain airports, regional level scaling mechanisms will be key to *accommodating* future needs for air transportation." (Paragraph 1)

    a. developing an understanding of
    b. increasing
    c. limiting
    d. providing enough for

2. "Initially, the air transportation network scales according to airport-level mechanisms—through the addition of capacity and the improvement of efficiency—but as infrastructure constraints are reached, higher-level scaling mechanisms such as the *emergence* of secondary airports and the construction of new high-capacity airports are triggered." (Paragraph 1)

    a. coming forward
    b. construction
    c. increase
    d. inefficiency

3. "With the growing demand for air transportation and the limited ability to increase capacity at key points in the air transportation system, there are concerns that, in the future, the system will not *scale* to meet demand." (Paragraph 2)

    a. adapt by growing
    b. be perceived properly
    c. be removed and replaced
    d. provide enough security

4. "Assuming a similar rate of growth to the rate of growth that *prevailed* between 1985 and 2005, passenger traffic would approach 1.9 billion RPKs by 2025." (Paragraph 2)

    a. was popular
    b. was predicted
    c. collapsed
    d. occurred

5. "However, infrastructure capacity constraints at airports create *congestion* that results in aircraft and passenger delays that propagate throughout the system." (Paragraph 2)

a. crowding
b. hesitation
c. inefficiency
d. limitation

6. "*Concurrently*, delays increased to reach a peak in 2000." (Paragraph 3)

a. as a result
b. in addition to this
c. at the highest
d. at the same time

7. "Given the growing demand for air transportation in the future and *inherent* key capacity constraints, there are concerns that, in the future, the system will not scale to meet demand." (Paragraph 4)

a. difficult to find
b. easy to see
c. built-in
d. left-out

8. "Because the primary and secondary airports that were identified in each of the regional airport system serves the demand for air transportation within the same region, these airports can be *aggregated into* one multi-airport system node." (Paragraph 15)

a. demolished by
b. combined into
c. misunderstood as
d. replaced by

9. "It was found that the average growth rate versus weight of the node in the network *deviates* from the linear relation for individual airports." (Paragraph 17)

a. differs
b. is calculated
c. is estimated
d. results

10. "In order to understand how the network evolves, an analysis of the scaling *mechanisms* and the factors that influence the structure of the network was performed." (Paragraph 25)

    a. details
    b. increases
    c. processes
    d. structures

Reading Focus

Connecting Sentences Using This *and* This + *Noun Phrase*

IDENTIFYING SENTENCE CONNECTIONS

In a reading, noun phrases beginning with **this** or **these** help connect ideas. For example, consider this passage from Paragraph 16:

> The presence of a power law distribution implies that there exists an underlying growth mechanism based on preferential attachment. This preferential attachment dynamic implies that a node grows proportionally to its size in the network (in an unconstrained case).

MAKING NOUN PHRASES WITH *THIS/THESE*

Complete each passage with an appropriate noun phrase. To fit the noun phrase you have supplied, circle either **this** or **these** and the proper form of the verb. The first one has been done for you as an example.

1. "Revenue passenger kilometers [RPK] have increased by a factor of 3.3 from 393 billion in 1978 to 1.304 billion in 2005." This /(These) _substantial increases_ is /(are) expected to continue as long as demand for air travel can continue to be met.

2. However, infrastructure capacity constraints at airports create congestion . . . **This / These** _____ **causes / cause** delays that affect airports throughout the air traffic network.

3. The events of September 11, 2001 led to a general slowdown of the economy. **This / These** _____ **was / were** responsible for a decrease in passengers flying in 2001 and 2002.

4. The demand for air transportation is increasing, while the system's capacity to provide air transportation is limited. **This / These** _____ **has / have** given rise to concerns that "in the future, the system will not scale to meet demand."

5. "[T]he air transportation system is fundamentally a network system (composed of thousands of interconnected subsystems and parts)." **This / These** _____ **mean / means** "it can be described and represented using network abstractions and tools from network theory."

6. "The ETMS traffic data showed that the frequency of flights on each U.S. flight route (ranging from 1 to 1000 flights per year) varied according to the kind of aircraft being flow." **This / These** _____ **show / shows** that "layers are not homogeneous in terms of both frequency and structure."

7. "Using historical data from the FAA Terminal Area Forecast database that covers the time period from 1976 to 2005, an analysis of the historical growth rate of airports was performed." **This / These** _____ **show / shows** "that the average growth rate versus weight of the node in the network deviates from the linear relation for individual airports."

8. "If the nodes had aligned with the hypothetical line, this would have indicated preferential attachment growth." However, several airports were observed to have deviated from a linear relationship. **This / These** _____ **is / are** "not surprising and" **was / were** "expected due to capacity constraints that limit the growth of certain airports."

9. "Over the last three decades, several key secondary airports have emerged in the United States serving demand for air transportation within a region." **This / These** _____ **has / have** provided passengers that live in secondary basins of population within a metropolitan region with an opportunity to "fly directly from a closer and less convoluted airport."

10. The 50-to-90 seat regional jets were introduced in the 1990s. **This / These** _____ **has / have** contributed to a trend of decreased average size of aircraft in the United States from 130 to 88 seats.

Parts of an Academic Journal Article

The reading by Bonnefoy and Hansman is from an academic journal. It is based on their analysis of data about the air-transport system in the United States. An academic journal article like this—a report of data analysis or some other kind of research—is likely to contain some or all of these parts:

- abstract—consolidates all main points of the article into one or two paragraphs <u>before</u> the main article

- information about the authors—names, places of employment, and other biographical information

- introduction—leads up to the main article

- methodology—explains how the authors conducted their analysis or research

- findings—lists facts discovered by the analysis or research

- discussion—explains the findings and puts them into a context

- conclusion—shows how the findings can lead to guesses about the situation being studied

- acknowledgments—thanks people or organizations who supported the study

- references—lists sources the authors consulted during their study

IDENTIFYING SECTIONS

Skim the reading. Write the numbers of the paragraph(s) corresponding to each part in the list. The first and last items are done for you. Discuss your answers with a partner or small group.

Part	Paragraph(s)
abstract	*1*
information about the authors	
introduction	
methodology	
findings	
discussion	
conclusion	
acknowledgments	
references	*After the text of the article*

MATCHING

Next to each section, write the letter(s) of any idea(s) found there. Not all sections are listed. A section may contain more than one idea, and an idea may be found in more than one section. Review the reading as much as necessary to find the answers. Discuss your answers with a partner or small group.

Section

1. abstract _____
2. methodology _____
3. findings _____
4. conclusions _____
5. acknowledgments _____
6. references _____

Idea

a. Some agencies of the U.S. federal government supported the authors' work.

b. Aircraft traffic data were used to model the network structure of U.S. air traffic.

c. A small number of airports account for most air traffic and the widest range of destinations, whereas a large number of airports have infrequent flights to limited destinations.

d. The authors consulted sources such as documents from the Federal Aviation Administration and the Bureau of Transportation Statistics.

e. Air traffic has increased in the past and led to increased delays. If that continues and airports cannot compensate for the increased demand, negative results will likely ensue.

f. Multiple airports serving a particular region can be considered a single multi-airport node in the air traffic network.

INTERPRETING AN ABSTRACT

An abstract summarizes ideas from various sections of the main text. In this article, the sections are marked with Roman numerals (I, II, etc.). The abstract is reproduced below. In the blank before each sentence, write the numeral(s) of the section(s) . A sentence may relate to more than one section, and a section may be represented by more than one sentence. The first two blanks are filled in for you as an example.

ABSTRACT

① _I_ With the growing demand for air transportation and the limited ability to increase capacity at key points in the air transportation system, there are concerns that, in the future, the system will not scale to meet demand. ② _I_. This situation will result in the generation and the propagation of delays throughout the system, impacting passengers' quality of travel and more broadly the economy. ③ _____ There is, therefore, the need to investigate the mechanisms by which the air transportation system scaled to meet demand in the past and will do so in the future. ④ _____ In order to investigate limits to scale of current air transportation networks, theories of scale-free and scalable networks were used. ⑤ _____ It was found that the U.S. air transportation network is not scalable at the airport level due to capacity constraints. ⑥ _____ However, the results of a case study analysis of multi-airport systems that led to the aggregation of these multiple airports into single nodes and the analysis of this network showed that the air transportation network was scalable at the regional level. ⑦ _____ In order to understand how the network evolves, an analysis of the scaling dynamics that influence the structure of the network was conducted. ⑧ _____ Initially, the air transportation network scales according to airport-level mechanisms—through the addition of capacity and the improvement of efficiency—but as infrastructure constraints are reached, higher-level scaling mechanisms such as the emergence of secondary airports and the construction of new high-capacity airports are triggered. ⑨ _____ These findings suggest that, given current and future limitations on the ability to add capacity at certain airports, regional-level scaling mechanisms will be key to accommodating future needs for air transportation.

Mistakes

Everyone makes mistakes. This unit looks at wrong-headed thinking and ill-considered behavior—and their often-catastrophic results. The unit is organized as follows:

- FIRST TIER: Hurricanes
  Book excerpt adapted from: **Audrey, Betsy, and Camille** by Ernest Zebrowski and Judith Howard

- SECOND TIER: The Destruction of an Entire Society
  Book chapter: **Why Do Some Societies Make Disastrous Decisions** by Jared Diamond

- THIRD TIER: Crime Spree
  Book chapter: **The Map Thief** by Miles Harvey

First Tier: Hurricanes

Pre-Reading

DISCUSSION

This reading deals with hurricanes. Before you read, discuss the questions in a small group. Use a dictionary and other reference sources as necessary.

1. In 2005, Hurricane Katrina hit the Gulf Coast of the United States and destroyed much of the city of New Orleans. Share what you know or have heard about the effects of this hurricane.

2. If you have Internet access, find something you didn't know about hurricanes in general—how they form, where they strike, etc.

3. Think about another natural disaster with which you are familiar. Were people prepared for it? How had they prepared? What kind of preparations would have improved the outcome? Share your knowledge and opinions.

Reading

Audrey, Betsy, and Camille

Hurricane Audrey, 1957

1 On June 25, 1957, the Weather Bureau (the predecessor of the National Weather Service) posted a hurricane watch for the Texas and Louisiana coasts. The name of the slow-moving storm that prompted the advisory, the first Atlantic storm of the 1957 season, was Audrey. At 10:00 a.m. on June 26, with the storm 117 miles from the coast and tracking north at 7.8 miles per hour, the Weather Bureau upgraded the hurricane watch to an official hurricane warning. Landfall, the meteorologists figured, would be in about 36 hours—late on the evening of June 27—and the most likely spot was Port Arthur on the Texas-Louisiana border. Early on the evening of June 26, Audrey intensified. She would soon enter the range of Houston's ground-based radar, and despite the primitive state of that technology in 1957, it would be possible to begin tracking the storm from land. Louisiana had no weather radar equipment whatsoever at that time, so the New Orleans branch of the Weather Bureau, which officially "owned" the storm, had to depend on Houston's interpretations of their radar blips.

2 Then, at around midnight on the 26th, the New Orleans office of the Weather Bureau got two pieces of horrifying information. First came a report that Audrey had intensified dramatically: she now had sustained winds of 135 miles per hour. Second, she was now racing toward the coast at 16 miles per hour and possibly even faster. Audrey would strike southwestern Louisiana early in the morning and with devastating winds.

3 Oblivious to the fact that there were but two routes north in all of Cameron Parish and just one way out of southwestern Vermilion Parish, the Weather Bureau issued a warning advising everyone in the low-lying areas to head inland at daybreak. By then, it was after midnight and most folks were asleep, confident that the hurricane was still a day away. Nor did it help that one radio station had a shift change that led the incoming announcer to repeat an earlier advisory when the new message slipped to the floor and lay there unnoticed. Many listeners got the impression that nothing at all had changed in the previous six hours and that the storm had stalled out in the Gulf. Others—particularly those Cajuns who in all their years had never developed a strong ear for the English language— had difficulty understanding the broadcasts through the rising levels of static on the AM-band radios that were still the norm in 1957.

4 The storm roared ashore in the pre-dawn darkness. The hundreds of dead—and thousands of injured and dispossessed—were victims not just of a natural phenomenon but also of an unfortunate confluence of human mistakes and oversights. Not only had the Weather Bureau's early warnings understated the danger, but inexperienced announcers at small rural radio stations delivered those advisories lackadaisically and sometimes inaccurately. Locally, there were no public emergency plans in place. Even if such plans had existed and the residents had been aware of them, they would have been useless unless some knowledgeable authority had contacted the local public officials directly. As it was, the local officials received no better advice or information than their constituents got directly from their own radios—information that ran late by six to 12 hours.

5 The catastrophe, of course, did nothing to enhance these rural folks' confidence in the distant federal bureaucracy that issued national hurricane forecasts. Even as the oil companies had been making correct and timely decisions to safeguard and evacuate their offshore platforms, the common citizens had been erroneously assured that they had another full day to prepare before Audrey's landfall. In the aftermath, many victims vilified the meteorologists as inept, overpaid, and unfamiliar with the regions their forecasts affected, and even lacking the courage to contritely visit the places where people had died because of their ineptitude. In Cameron Parish, a group of angry survivors banded together to bring a

class-action lawsuit against the Weather Bureau and the radio stations. But, nine days after the disaster, every tape and transcript of the local stations' weather announcements mysteriously disappeared. Lacking the necessary evidence, and in the face of the Weather Bureau's virtually impregnable claim of legal immunity, the lawsuits never progressed.

Hurricane Camille, 1969

6 Some lessons learned from Audrey—and from a 1965 storm named Betsy—shaped the response of Gulf Coast residents when an entirely different kind of storm spun up in the Gulf in August, 1969. Its name was Camille.

7 Distrust of outside authorities was an established credo of local politicians and residents by the time of Camille, but it was nothing new. It had already sunk deep roots into the region even before Audrey. That storm simply confirmed it, and linked it inseparably to the weather, as did subsequent hurricanes. Motivated by this suspicion and by a bloated faith in their own abilities, local authorities tended to make stupid decisions. For example, after Betsy struck in 1965, Leander Perez, the top official in Plaquemines Parish, Louisiana, sealed off his territory and would not let anyone in by road—no insurance adjusters, no journalists, not even the Louisiana National Guard. Only when his emergency-response chief pointed out the threat of looters did Perez reluctantly allow the governor to send in the Guard. Even then, Perez insisted that they follow his orders, not the governor's.

8 But there were also beneficial effects of local skepticism, especially to the extent that citizens took charge where government famously faltered. Weather forecasting was not at all the same pursuit in 1969 as it had been 12 years earlier. By 1969, 18 weather satellites had been launched into orbit and five were still functioning. Camille would become the first hurricane they photographed from birth through death. But this advance did not mean all was well with hurricane forecasts by the National Weather Service. The photographs, not very good to begin with, were corrupted by analog equipment that distributed them to field offices. The photographs also lacked accurate reference points to identify latitude and longitude. This had to be done manually, a process that often resulted in errors of 50 miles or more in pinpointing the center of a storm. The most serious shortcoming, however, was that the photos from space showed only the tops of the clouds, which were about eight miles above what really mattered—the action at the surface. The net result was that an uncritical reliance on Weather Service forecasts was still a mistake.

9 One of the few constitutionally mandated responsibilities of the Mississippi governor's office is emergency preparedness. The governor in

1969, Ross Barnett, could be counted on to neglect this important task just as egregiously as had every previous Mississippi governor. When Hurricane Betsy pummeled Hancock County, Mississippi, no one in the office of the governor, Paul B. Johnson, Jr., seemed to have the foggiest clue of what to do. But those public servants did not view their ignorance as their own fault; after all, they and Johnson had only been in charge for eight months.

10 For a few insightful people in the coastal counties, Betsy was a call to action. If there was ever going to be any meaningful emergency planning for the coast, it would need to be initiated and implemented by the coastal residents themselves. The state officials up in Jackson were too out of touch to accomplish anything of any real value related to disaster planning for the coast.

11 In Biloxi, Mississippi, Julia and Wade Guice, local businesspeople, embarked on a mission: to draw together a network of coastal police departments, fire units, health workers, radio broadcasters, tow-truck companies, clergy, and countless other volunteers to plan out a coordinated response to the next big hurricane, whenever it might occur.

12 On August 17, 1969, Hurricane Camille made landfall in southeast Louisiana, near New Orleans and the mouth of the Mississippi River. Of all hurricanes to hit the United States since 1900 (including Hurricane Katrina in 2005), Camille had the highest recorded sustained winds (172 miles per hour) at landfall. It was also one of only three Category 5 hurricanes—the strongest type—to hit the U.S. since 1900. Hurricane Katrina, by comparison, was a Category 4 storm.

13 About 340 people are known to have died because of Camille— almost all of them in the states of Louisiana, Mississippi, and Virginia. Camille's death toll, though tragic, was remarkably low considering the violence of the storm. Although it might be supposed that compiling statistics on disaster fatalities accomplishes little beyond satisfying morbid curiosity, the death toll from the disaster informs us, at the very least, about the effectiveness of emergency planning and hazard mitigation.

14 On the oil platforms offshore in the Gulf of Mexico, where every one of the thousands of workers was taken off in a timely manner, there were no fatalities at all. In Plaquemines Parish, Luke Petrovich, the emergency-preparedness officer, issued an evacuation order early. Virtually everybody evacuated the lower peninsula, and there were only seven deaths—less than one fatality per 2,500 residents. Along the Mississippi coast, more than 85,000 people evacuated—mostly in compliance with the voluntary plan cobbled together by the Guices and other community leaders—and another 50,000 or so took at least some steps to prepare themselves. As a consequence, fewer than 200 died, a mortality ratio of less than one death

per 700 natives. In Nelson County, Virginia, however, where no evacuation warning was possible, the death rate exceeded one fatality per 100 county residents.

15 The obvious lesson is that lives indeed are saved when local officials and at-risk residents have time to prepare. Proper preparation, however, requires knowledge that cannot be generated using local resources alone. Despite all their errors in the past, the National Weather Service, the National Hurricane Center, and the Army Corps of Engineers (which monitors the river gauges) are essential national resources, worthy of taxpayer support, even by those who might otherwise oppose "big government."

Post-Reading
Basic Comprehension

MULTIPLE CHOICE

Circle the choice that best answers each question.

1. Which statement best expresses the main idea of the reading?
   a. Hurricane Audrey caused much greater damage on the Gulf Coast than did Hurricane Camille.
   b. Improved technology for tracking, measuring, and predicting hurricanes has led to great improvements in hurricane preparedness.
   c. Nature is a force beyond human control, so no matter how well people prepare for natural disasters, fatalities are inevitable.
   d. Preparation at a local level can save lives, but cooperation between local and national organizations is also required.

2. Which was NOT mentioned as a factor contributing to the failure to evacuate before Hurricane Audrey?
   a. a sudden change in the hurricane's direction
   b. errors in broadcast reports
   c. some listeners' inability to understand English well
   d. static on the radio

3. What can be inferred from Paragraph 3 about some Cajuns?

    a. They could not afford high-quality radios.

    b. They had recently arrived in Louisiana from another country.

    c. They had long lived in Louisiana but sometimes had trouble with English.

    d. They seldom had contact with other people in Louisiana.

4. Which word best describes local sentiment toward federal institutions in the aftermath of Audrey?

    a. approving

    b. ashamed

    c. confident

    d. mistrustful

5. What is the purpose of the anecdote about Leander Perez in Paragraph 7?

    a. To illustrate how suspicious local politicians were

    b. To demonstrate the importance of institutions such as the National Guard

    c. To criticize federal responses to Betsy

    d. To provide an example of ineffective hurricane preparations

6. What was true of satellites that monitored storms in 1969?

    a. Eighteen were in operation at the time of Hurricane Camille.

    b. They identified the location of Camille precisely.

    c. They took pictures of Camille from beginning to end.

    d. They showed the clouds that made up Camille from top to bottom.

7. Which of the following best explains the main idea of Paragraph 9?

    a. The Mississippi governor's office is responsible for emergency preparedness.

    b. The Mississippi governor's office was inept when it came to dealing with Hurricane Betsy.

    c. The public servants were not at fault because they had only been in office for a short time.

    d. Ross Barnett was a less competent governor than his predecessors.

8. Which is NOT mentioned as being helpful in dealing with Camille?

   a. a National Guard evacuation unit
   b. an emergency preparedness officer
   c. local businesspeople
   d. local residents

9. Based on the information provided in the reading, which storm probably had the most powerful winds?

   a. Audrey
   b. Betsy
   c. Camille
   d. Katrina

COMPLETING A CHART

Six of the following eight sentences are related to either Audrey or Camille, as discussed in the reading. Write the letter of each sentence under the name of the hurricane it describes. Two of the answer choices will NOT be used.

It resulted in a relatively low number of fatalities.

It was tracked by ground-based radar.

It was tracked by satellite.

It struck Louisiana, Mississippi, and Virginia.

Its winds were greater than 175 miles per hour.

Local populations prepared for it in advance.

No one was evacuated before it struck.

Warnings about it arrived too late.

Hurricane Audrey	Hurricane Camille

MAP WORK

Look at the map of the area mentioned in the reading.

1. Fill in the blanks on the map with the names of the places listed.
2. Trace the path of Hurricane Audrey on the map.
3. Mark the areas affected by Hurricanes Betsy and Camille.

Biloxi, Mississippi	Jackson, Mississippi	Plaquemines Parish
Cameron Parish	Nelson County	Port Arthur
Hancock County	New Orleans, Louisiana	Vermilion Parish

SHORT ANSWER

Use information from the reading to answer the questions in your own words.

1. How can local leaders help make disaster-preparedness efforts successful?_____

    _____

    _____

2. How can local leaders contribute to the failure of disaster-preparedness efforts?_____

    _____

    _____

Vocabulary

MULTIPLE CHOICE

Circle the choice that best answers the questions. Use the context of the reading and a dictionary as necessary.

1. Which of the following is closest in meaning to *whatsoever* (Paragraph 1)?

   a. at all
   b. available
   c. earlier than
   d. or things like that

2. Which of the following is closest in meaning to *intensified* (Paragraph 1 and 2)?

   a. became more frightening
   b. became stronger
   c. came closer
   d. shifted direction

3. Which of the following is closest in meaning to *oblivious to* (Paragraph 3)?

   a. because of
   b. in spite of
   c. keeping track of
   d. unaware of

4. Which of the following is closest in meaning to *oversights* (Paragraph 4)?

   a. things that occur in nature
   b. things someone has responsibility for
   c. things someone accidentally missed
   d. things that produce good results

5. Which of the following is closest in meaning to *understated* (Paragraph 4)?

   a. misinterpreted [the danger]
   b. reduced the intensity of [the danger]
   c. said [the danger] was less than it really was
   d. stated [the danger] in simple terms

6. Which of the following is closest in meaning to *subsequent* (Paragraph 7)?

   a. came later
   b. less powerful
   c. lower-lying
   d. previous

7. Which of the following is closest in meaning to *corrupted* (Paragraph 8)?

   a. distorted
   b. misused
   c. enlarged
   d. taken

8. Which of the following is closest in meaning to *the foggiest clue* (Paragraph 9)?

   a. an unclear understanding
   b. any idea
   c. good insight
   d. knowledge about weather

9. Which of the following is closest in meaning to *death toll* (Paragraph 13)?

   a. the number of people killed
   b. money charged for rebuilding after a disaster
   c. power to cause death
   d. taxes lost due to fatalities

10. Which of the following is closest in meaning to *fatalities* (Paragraph 14)?

    a. damaged machines
    b. emergency plans
    c. losses of life
    d. health problems

11. Which of the following is closest in meaning to *generated* (Paragraph 15)?

    a. understood
    b. improved upon
    c. increased in power
    d. created

MATCHING

Match each italicized word or phrase on the left with the word or phrase on the right that most closely relates to it.

1. a tool used for *tracking* weather (Paragraph 1) ____

2. a situation in which you might hear *static* (Paragraph 3) ____

3. a situation in which people are *dispossessed* (Paragraph 4) ____

4. the governor of Louisiana's *constituents* (Paragraph 4) ____

5. a place that you hope is *impregnable* (Paragraph 5) ____

6. a situation that you might treat with *skepticism* (Paragraph 8) ____

7. someone you can *count on* to tell you the truth (Paragraph 9) ____

8. a situation in which people are satisfying *morbid curiosity* (Paragraph 13) ____

9. people who are not *in compliance* with regulations (Paragraph 14) ____

10. a way of *generating* ideas (Paragraph 15) ____

a. after an earthquake has destroyed homes

b. brainstorming

c. radar

d. smokers smoking in a no-smoking area

e. the bank vault where your money is kept

f. the state's residents

g. when people crowd around to look at the victims of a traffic accident

h. when the TV is tuned to a station that isn't broadcasting

i. when your friend tells you about being taken by aliens aboard a UFO

j. your most trusted friend

GOVERNMENT AND CULTURAL TERMS

Write the meaning of each term. Use a dictionary, the Internet, or other resources as necessary.

Army Corps of Engineers _____

_____

class-action lawsuit _____

_____

clergy _____

_____

county _____

_____

governor _____

_____

insurance adjuster _____

_____

National Guard _____

_____

National Hurricane Center _____

_____

National Weather Service _____

_____

parish _____

_____

Weather Bureau _____

_____

Reading Focus
Putting Reading to Work

WRITING AND DISCUSSION

Read the items and complete the research assignments.

1. The reading mentions four hurricanes by name: Audrey, Betsy, Camille, and Katrina. These are names given to people as well. How are hurricanes named, and why are particular names chosen? Using outside sources, write a paragraph that answers these questions. Use your own words.

2. Think of a natural disaster that was dealt with effectively by local or national governments. Answer as many of the questions as you can.

   - What happened? How many people were affected? How were they affected?
   - What kind of planning and preparation had the local area done?
   - What kind of planning and preparation had the national government done?
   - What did local people do to speed recovery?
   - How did national organizations assist in recovery?

3. Think of a natural disaster that was NOT dealt with effectively by local or national governments. Use the same questions as guidelines. Comment on other aspects of the disaster if they seem important.

4. Compare the situations you wrote about and discussed in questions 1–3. Write a three-paragraph essay or prepare a five-minute oral presentation contrasting the two situations.

Second Tier: The Destruction of an Entire Society

Pre-Reading

Discussion

Tier 1 covered some cases where communities' lack of preparation for natural disasters led to tragedy. These communities, however, recovered eventually. Other communities in history have disappeared as a result of a disaster.

1. Can you think of any examples in history when a community or society was not able to recover from a calamity?
2. Why couldn't the community recover?

Before you read, discuss the questions in a small group.

Reading

Why Do Some Societies Make Disastrous Decisions?[1]

1 My first lecture was on the collapse of Easter Island society. In the class discussion after I had finished my presentation, the apparently simple question that most puzzled my students was one whose actual complexity hadn't sunk into me before: how on earth could a society make such an obviously disastrous decision as to cut down all the trees on which it depended? One of the students asked what I thought the islander who cut down the last palm tree said as he was doing it. For every other society that I treated in subsequent lectures, my students raised essentially the same ques-

tion. They also asked the related question: how often did people wreak ecological damage intentionally, or at least while aware of the likely consequences? How often did people instead do it without meaning to, or out of ignorance? My students wondered whether—if there are still people left alive a hundred years from now—those people of the next century will be as astonished about our blindness today as we are about the blindness of the Easter Islanders.

2 This question of why societies end up destroying themselves through disastrous decisions aston-

---

[1]"Why Do Some Societies Make Disastrous Decisions?" from *Collapse: How Societies Choose to Fail or Succeed* by Jared Diamond, copyright © 2005 by Jared Diamond. Used by permission of Viking Penguin, a division of the Penguin Group (USA) Inc.

ishes not only my UCLA undergraduates but also professional historians and archaeologists. For example, the archaeologist Joseph Tainter's reasoning suggested to him that complex societies are not likely to allow themselves to collapse through failure to manage their environmental resources. Yet it is clear that precisely such a failure has happened repeatedly. How did so many societies make such bad mistakes?

3 My UCLA undergraduates, and Joseph Tainter as well, have identified a baffling phenomenon: namely, failures of group decision-making on the part of whole societies or other groups. That problem is, of course, related to the problem of failures of individual decision-making. Individuals, too, make bad decisions: they enter bad marriages, they make bad investments and career choices, their businesses fail, and so on. But some additional factors enter into failures of group decision-making, such as conflicts of interest among members of the group and group dynamics. This is obviously a complex subject to which there would not be a single answer fitting all situations.

4 What I'm going to propose instead is a road map of factors contributing to failures of group decision-making. First of all, a group may fail to anticipate a problem before the problem actually arrives. Second, when the problem does arrive, the group may fail to perceive it. While all this discussion of reasons for failure and societal collapses may seem depressing, the flip side is a heartening subject: namely, successful decision-making. Perhaps if we understood the reasons why groups often make bad decisions, we could use that knowledge as a checklist to guide groups to make good decisions.

5 Groups may do disastrous things because they failed to anticipate a problem before it arrives, for any of several reasons. One is that they may have had no prior experience of any such problems, and so may not have been sensitized to the possibility.

6 A prime example is the mess that British colonists created for themselves when they introduced foxes and rabbits from Britain into Australia in the 1800s. Today these rate as two of the most disastrous examples of impacts of alien species on an environment to which they were not native. These introductions are all the more tragic because they were carried out intentionally at much effort, rather than resulting inadvertently from tiny seeds overlooked in transported hay, as in so many cases of establishment of noxious weeds. Foxes have proceeded to prey on and exterminate many species of native Australian mammals without evolutionary experience of foxes, while rabbits consume much of the plant fodder intended for sheep and cattle, outcompete native herbivorous

mammals, and undermine the ground by their burrows.

7 With the gift of hindsight, we now view it as incredibly stupid that colonists would intentionally release into Australia two alien mammals that have caused billions of dollars in damages and expenditures to control them. We recognize today, from many other such examples, that introductions often prove disastrous in unexpected ways. That's why, when you go to Australia or the U.S. as a visitor or returning resident, one of the first questions you are now asked by immigration officers is whether you are carrying any plants, seeds, or animals—to reduce the risk of their escaping and becoming established. From abundant prior experience we have now learned (often but not always) to anticipate at least the potential dangers of introducing species. But it's still difficult even for professional ecologists to predict which introductions will actually become established, which established successful introductions will prove disastrous, and why the same species establishes itself at certain sites of introduction and not at others. Hence we really shouldn't be surprised that 19th century Australians, lacking the 20th century's experience of disastrous introductions, failed to anticipate the effects of rabbits and foxes.

8 We have encountered other examples of societies understandably failing to anticipate a problem of which they lacked prior experience. Investing heavily in walrus hunting in order to export walrus ivory to Europe, the Greenland Norse could hardly have anticipated that the Crusades would eliminate the market for walrus ivory by reopening Europe's access to Asian and African elephant ivory, or that increasing sea ice would impede ship traffic to Europe. Again, not being soil scientists, the Maya at Copan could not foresee that deforestation of the hill slopes would trigger soil erosion from the slopes into the valley bottoms.

9 Even prior experience is not a guarantee that a society will anticipate a problem, if the experience happened so long ago as to have been forgotten. That's especially a problem for non-literate societies, which have less capacity than literate societies to preserve detailed memories of events long in the past because of the limitations of oral transmission of information compared to writing. For instance, Chaco Canyon Anasazi society survived several droughts before succumbing to a big drought in the 20th century AD. But the earlier droughts had occurred long before the birth of any Anasazi affected by the big drought, which would thus have been unanticipated because the Anasazi lacked writing. Similarly, the Classic Lowland Maya succumbed to a drought in the 9th century, despite their area having been affected by drought centuries earlier. In that case, although the

Maya did have writing, it recorded kings' deeds and astronomical events rather than weather reports, so that the drought of the 3rd century did not help the Maya anticipate the drought of the 9th century.

10 In modern literate societies whose writing does discuss subjects besides kings and planets, that doesn't necessarily mean that we draw on prior experience committed to writing. We, too, tend to forget things. For a year or two after the gas shortages of the 1973 Gulf oil crisis, we Americans shied away from gas-guzzling cars, but then we forgot that experience and are now embracing SUVs, despite volumes of print spilled over the 1973 events. When the city of Tucson in Arizona went through a severe drought in the 1950s, its alarmed citizens swore they would manage their water better, but soon returned to their water-guzzling ways of building golf courses and watering their gardens.

11 Another reason why a society may fail to anticipate a problem involves reasoning by false analogy. When we are in an unfamiliar situation, we fall back on drawing analogies with old familiar situations. That's a good way to proceed if the old and new situations are truly analogies, but it can be dangerous if they are only superficially similar. For instance, Vikings who immigrated to Iceland beginning around the year AD 870 arrived from Norway and Britain, which have heavy clay soils ground up by gla-ciers. Even if the vegetation covering those soils is cleared, the spoils themselves are too heavy to be blown away. When the Viking colonists encountered in Iceland many of the same tree species already familiar to them from Norway and Britain, they were deceived by the apparent similarity of the landscape. Unfortunately, Iceland's soils arose not through glacial grinding but through winds carrying light ash blown out in volcanic eruptions. Once the Vikings had cleared Iceland's forests to create pastures for their livestock, the light soil became exposed for the wind to blow out again, and much of Iceland's topsoil soon eroded away.

12 A tragic and famous modern example of reasoning by false analogy involves French military preparations from World War II. After the horrible bloodbath of World War I, France recognized its vital need to protect itself against the possibility of another German invasion. Unfortunately, the French army staff assumed that a next war would be fought similarly to World War I, in which the Western Front between France and Germany had remained locked in static trench warfare for four years. Defensive infantry forces manning elaborate fortified trenches had usually been able to repel infantry attacks, while offensive forces had deployed the newly invented tanks only individually and just in support of attacking infantry. Hence, France constructed an even

more elaborate and expensive system of fortifications, the Maginot Line, to guard its eastern frontier against Germany. But the German army staff, having been defeated in World War I, recognized the need for a different strategy. It used tanks rather than infantry to spearhead its attacks, massed the tanks into separate armored divisions, bypassed the Maginot Line through forested terrain previously considered unsuitable for tanks, and thereby defeated France within a mere six weeks. In reasoning by false analogy after World War I, French generals made a common mistake: generals often plan for a coming war as if it will be like the previous war, especially if that previous war was one in which their side was victorious.

13 The second stop on my road map, after a society has or hasn't anticipated a problem before it arrives, involves its perceiving or failing to perceive a problem that has actually arrived. There are at least three reasons for such failures, all of them common in the business world and academia.

14 First, the origins of some problems are literally imperceptible. For example, the nutrients responsible for soil fertility are invisible to the eye, and only in modern times did they become measurable by chemical analysis. In Australia, Mangareva, parts of the U.S. Southwest, and many other locations, most of the nutrients had already been leeched from the soil by rain before human settlement. When people arrived and began growing crops, those crops quickly exhausted the remaining nutrients, and as a result, agriculture failed. Yet such nutrient-poor soils often bear lush-appearing vegetation. It's just that most of the nutrients in the ecosystem are contained in the vegetation rather than in the soil, and are removed if one cuts down the vegetation. There was no way for the first colonists of Australia and Mangareva to perceive that problem of soil nutrient exhaustion—nor for farmers in areas with salt deep in the ground (like eastern Montana and parts of Australia and Mesopotamia) to perceive incipient salinization—nor for miners of sulfide ores to perceive the toxic copper and acid dissolved in mine runoff water.

15 Another frequent reason for failure to perceive a problem after it has arrived is distant managers, a potential issue in any large society or business. For example, the largest private landowner and timber company in Montana today is based not within that state but 400 miles away in Seattle, Washington. Not being on the scene, company executives may not realize that they have a big weed problem on their forest properties. Well-run companies avoid such surprises by periodically sending managers "into the field" to observe what is actually going on, while a tall friend of mine who was a college

president regularly practiced with his school's undergraduates on their basketball courts in order to keep abreast of student thinking. The opposite of failure due to distant managers is success due to on-the-spot managers. Part of the reason Tikopians on their tiny island, and New Guinea highlanders in their valleys, have successfully managed their resources for more than a thousand years is that everyone on the island or in the valley is familiar with the entire territory on which their society depends.

16 Perhaps the commonest circumstance under which societies fail to perceive a problem is when it takes the form of a slow trend concealed by wide up-and-down fluctuations. The prime example in modern times is global warming. We now realize that temperatures around the world have been slowly rising in recent decades, due in large part to atmospheric changes caused by humans. However, it is not the case that the climate each year has been exactly 0.01 degree warmer than in the previous year. Instead, as we all know, climate fluctuates up and down erratically from year to year; three degrees warmer in one summer than in the previous summer, then two degrees warmer the next summer, down four degrees the following summer, down another degree the next one, then up five degrees, etc. With such large and unpredictable fluctuations, it has taken a long time to discern the average upwards trend of 0.01 degree per year within that noisy signal. That's why it was only a few years ago that most professional climatologists previously skeptical of the reality of global warming became convinced. As I write these lines, President Bush of the U.S. is still not convinced of its reality, and he thinks we need more research. The medieval Greenlanders had similar difficulties in recognizing that their climate was gradually becoming colder, and the Maya and Anasazi had trouble discerning that theirs was becoming drier.

17 Politicians use the term "creeping normalcy" to refer to such slow trends concealed within noisy fluctuations. If the economy, schools, traffic congestion, or anything else is deteriorating only slowly, it's difficult to recognize that each successive year is on the average slightly worse than the year before, so one's baseline standard for what constitutes "normalcy" shifts gradually and imperceptibly. It may take a few decades of a long sequence of such slight year-to-year changes before people realize, with a jolt, that conditions used to be much better several decades ago, and that what is accepted as normalcy has crept downwards.

18 Another term related to creeping normalcy is "landscape amnesia": forgetting how different the surrounding landscape looked 50 years ago, because the change

from year to year has been so gradual. An example involves the melting of Montana's glaciers and snowfields caused by global warming. . . . After spending the summers of 1953 and 1956 in Montana's Big Hole Basin as a teenager, I did not return until 42 years later, in 1998, when I began visiting every year. Among my vivid teenaged memories of the Big Hole were the snow covering the distant mountaintops even in mid-summer, my resulting sense that a white band low in the sky encircled the basin, and my recollection of a weekend camping trip when two friends and I clambered up to that magical band of snow. Not having lived through the fluctuations and gradual dwindling of summer snow during the intervening 42 years, I was stunned and saddened on my return to the Big Hole in 1998 to find the band almost gone, and in 2001 and 2003 actually all melted off. When I asked my Montana resident friends about the change, they were less aware of it: they unconsciously compared each year's band (or lack thereof) with the previous few years. Creeping normalcy or landscape amnesia made it harder for them than for me to remember what conditions had been like in the 1950s. Such experiences are a major reason why people may fail to notice a developing problem, until it is too late.

19 I suspect that landscape amnesia provided part of the answer to my UCLA student's question, "What did the Easter Islander who cut down the last palm tree say as he was doing it?" We unconsciously imagine a sudden change: one year, the island still covered with a forest of tall palm trees being used to produce wine, fruit, and timber to transport and erect statues; the next year, just a single tree left, which an islander proceeds to fell in an act of incredibly self-damaging stupidity. Much more likely, though, the changes in forest cover from year to year would have been almost undetectable: yes, this year we cut down a few trees over there, but saplings are starting to grow back again here on this abandoned garden site. Only the oldest islanders, thinking back to their childhoods decades earlier, could have recognized a difference. The children could no more have comprehended their parents' tales of a tall forest than my 17-year-old sons today can comprehend my wife's and my tales of what Los Angeles used to be like 40 years ago. Gradually, Easter Island's trees became fewer, smaller, and less important. At the time that the last fruit-bearing adult palm tree was cut, the species had long ago ceased to be of any economic significance. That left only smaller and smaller palm saplings to clear each year, along with other bushes and treelets. No one would have noticed the falling of the last little palm sapling. By then, the memory of the valuable palm forest of centuries earlier had succumbed to landscape amnesia.

Conversely, the speed with which deforestation spread over early Tokugawa, Japan, made it easier for its shoguns to recognize the landscape changes and the need for preemptive action.

* * *

20 Societies often fail even to attempt to solve a problem once it has been perceived. Many reasons for this fall under the heading of what economists and other social scientists term "rational behavior," arising from clashes of interest among people. That is, some people may reason correctly that they can advance their own interests by behavior harmful to other people. Scientists term such behavior "rational" precisely because it employs correct reasoning, even though it might be morally reprehensible. The perpetrators know they will often get away with their bad behavior especially if there is no law against it or if the law isn't effectively enforced.

21 A frequent type of rational bad behavior is "good for me, bad for you and everybody else"—to put it bluntly, "selfishness." As a simple example, most Montana fishermen fish for trout. A few fishermen who prefer to fish for pike, a larger, fish-eating fish not native to western Montana, surreptitiously and illegally introduced pike to some western Montana lakes and rivers, where they proceeded to destroy trout fishing by eating out the trout. This was good for the few pike fishermen and bad for the far greater number of trout fishermen.

22 Another type of behavior that is rational but wrongheaded sets in when the interests of the decision-making elite in power clash with the interests of the rest of society. Especially if the elite can insulate themselves from the consequences of their actions, they are likely to do things that profit themselves, regardless of whether those actions hurt everybody else. Such clashes are becoming increasingly frequent in the U.S., where rich people tend to live in their gated compounds and drink bottled water. Throughout recorded history, actions or inactions by self-absorbed kings, chiefs, and politicians have been a regular cause of societal collapses, including those of the Maya kings, Greenland Norse chiefs, and modern Rwandan politicians.

23 Other failures to attempt to solve perceived problems involve what social scientists consider "irrational behavior": i.e., behavior that is harmful for everybody. Such irrational behavior often arises when each of us individually is torn by clashes of values: we may ignore a bad status quo because it is favored by some deeply held value to which we cling. Psychologists use the term "sunk-cost effect" for a related trait: we feel reluctant to abandon a policy (or sell a stock) in which we have already invested heavily.

24 Religious values tend to be especially deeply held and hence frequent causes of disastrous behavior. For example, much of the deforestation of Easter Island had a religious motivation: to obtain logs to transport and erect the giant stone statues that were the object of veneration.

25 It is painfully difficult to decide whether to abandon some of one's core values when they seem to be becoming incompatible with survival. At what point do we as individuals prefer to die rather than to compromise and live? All such decisions involve gambles, because one often can't be certain that clinging to core values will be fatal, or (conversely) that abandoning them will ensure survival. In trying to carry on as Christian farmers, the Greenland Norse in effect were deciding that they were prepared to die as Christian farmers rather than live as Inuit; they lost that gamble.

26 Common further irrational motives for failure to address problems include that the public may widely dislike those who first perceive and complain about the problem—such as Tasmania's Green Party that first protested foxes' introduction into Tasmania. The public may dismiss warnings because previous warnings proved to be false alarms, as illustrated by Aesop's fable about the eventual fate of the shepherd boy who had repeatedly cried, "Wolf!" and whose cries for help were then ignored when a wolf did appear. The public may shirk responsibility by invoking ISEP— "It's someone else's problem."

Post-Reading

Basic Comprehension

MULTIPLE CHOICE

Circle the choice that best answers the questions.

1. Paragraph 1 suggests that Diamond's lecture on Easter Island society concluded that the collapse of Easter Island society was caused by _____.

   a. a set of complex natural disasters
   b. outsiders who caused ecological damage
   c. the cutting down of palm trees
   d. the poor eyesight of the Easter Islanders

2. Which of the following is NOT mentioned as a negative consequence of the introduction of foxes and rabbits to Australia?

   a. Rabbits competed with cattle for food.
   b. Rabbits ate the food of native animals.
   c. Foxes killed native animals.
   d. The animals carried harmful seeds in their fur.

3. How does the discussion of Americans' current embrace of SUVs support the author's point in Paragraph 10?

   a. It shows how modern technology is superior to that of the Anasazi and the Maya.
   b. It shows how even literate societies can fail to anticipate a problem in spite of prior experience.
   c. It shows differences between the 1973 Gulf oil crisis and more recent crises.
   d. It shows that gasoline prices do not stay high for very long.

4. Which statement best describes "reasoning by false analogy" (Paragraph 11)?

   a. A similar problem has never happened to that society before.
   b. The society incorrectly compares the situation to another similar situation.
   c. The society's written history concentrates on the deeds of kings.
   d. There is no written record of a similar problem in the society's history.

5. According to the reading, why were the French preparations following World War I insufficient?

   a. Elaborate fortified trenches were so expensive that France could not buy tanks.

   b. The Germans had tanks but the French didn't.

   c. The Maginot Line went through forests that made tanks hard to use.

   d. The Germans used their tanks differently than they had during World War I.

6. Which of the following is NOT mentioned as a reason why societies fail to notice problems that are already occurring?

   a. Managers are far from the problem areas.

   b. People move too often to become familiar with any landscape.

   c. People lack sufficiently advanced scientific knowledge.

   d. People overlook gradual trends as they focus on year-to-year change.

7. When people began growing crops in Australia, Mangareva, and parts of the U.S. Southwest, they removed vegetation. How did this harm the soil?

   a. Salt in the area dried up and blew away.

   b. It made soil nutrients sink too deep for plants to reach with their roots.

   c. It caused rainfall to increase, which flooded the land.

   d. It removed most nutrients because they were stored in the vegetation, not in the soil.

8. According to the reading, which statement partially explains why people failed to notice global warming until recently?

   a. Actual temperatures from one year to the next do not necessarily increase.

   b. Political leaders discouraged climatologists from doing sufficient research.

   c. Temperatures vary considerably from place to place around the world.

   d. The average temperature over large periods of time has not increased.

9. Which is the best definition of *creeping normalcy* (Paragraph 17)?

   a. a political strategy for improving conditions that have deteriorated
   b. a sudden realization that conditions were better several decades ago
   c. failure to recognize that a change is occurring because it occurs so slowly
   d. the tendency for economics, education, traffic, etc. to become worse over time

10. Which statement describes how Diamond's Montana friends suffer from "landscape amnesia"?

   a. The group of people he used to camp with gradually dwindled until no one remembered their trips.
   b. As cities grew bigger, his friends forgot what an undeveloped landscape looked like.
   c. The snow covering the mountaintops decreased only slightly from year to year, so they didn't notice it.
   d. They paid no attention to the natural beauty in their everyday surroundings.

11. Which of the following is NOT mentioned as a reason why societies avoid trying to solve problems?

   a. educational systems that discourage "rational behavior"
   b. differences between the interests of the upper-class and those of the rest of society
   c. the perception that the problems are someone else's responsibility
   d. religious values that are regarded as more important than environmental issues

12. What can be inferred from Paragraph 26 about Tasmania's Green Party?

   a. It did not consider the problem of introducing foxes until too late.
   b. It opposed the introduction of foxes because it wanted to protect rabbits.
   c. It was not liked by many of the Tasmanian people.
   d. It was the dominant political party at the time

Vocabulary

MULTIPLE CHOICE

Circle the choice that best answers each question.

1. Which of the following is closest in meaning to *astonished* (Paragraph 1)?

    a. amused
    b. interested
    c. unconcerned
    d. very surprised

2. Which of the following is closest in meaning to *anticipate* (Paragraphs 4 and 5)?

    a. cause
    b. predict
    c. solve
    d. understand

3. Which of the following is closest in meaning to *established* (Paragraph 7)?

    a. stable and able to increase in population
    b. infesting
    c. harmful to members of other species
    d. well known

4. Which of the following is closest in meaning to *prior* (Paragraphs 8 and 9)?

    a. earlier
    b. positive
    c. sufficient
    d. written

5. Which of the following is closest in meaning to *keep abreast of* (Paragraph 15)?

    a. learn to understand
    b. maintain current knowledge about
    c. predict the fate of
    d. stay in shape with

6. Which of the following is closest in meaning to *reprehensible* (Paragraph 20)?

   a. respectable
   b. questionable
   c. objectionable
   d. understandable

7. Which of the following is closest in meaning to *surreptitiously* (Paragraph 21)?

   a. largely
   b. selfishly
   c. repeatedly
   d. secretly

8. Which of the following is closest in meaning to *status quo* (Paragraph 23)?

   a. behavior
   b. investment opportunity
   c. current situation
   d. reputation

9. Which of the following is closest in meaning to *carry on* (Paragraph 25)?

   a. complain
   b. continue
   c. improve
   d. spread

10. Which of the following is closest in meaning to *shirk* (Paragraph 26)?

   a. announce
   b. avoid
   c. destroy
   d. mistake

PARAPHRASING

Using the best key vocabulary item from the list, rephrase each statement. Change as much of the original as necessary to use the item you have chosen, but do not change the meaning of the original. Use each item from the list only once.

abundant	imperceptible	intentionally
anticipate	inadvertently	succumb
draw on	incipient	veneration
fluctuation		

1. Of course, societies don't set out to destroy themselves on purpose, but nevertheless, it is the decisions they make that, in many cases, lead to their destruction.

   _____

2. The mining process accidentally released toxic chemicals into nearby waterways.

   _____

3. Because of the introduction of foreign species, previously plentiful native species became scarce.

   _____

4. If a society has faced a similar problem in the past, it may be able to think about future problems in advance and work to prevent them.

   _____

5. The Greenland Norse of the 15th century are believed to have died out under the pressure of starvation, but the actual cause of their demise is uncertain.

   _____

6. Literate societies are able to gain information from the experience of previous generations more effectively than non-literate societies.

   _____

7. Each year, the glacier melts by an amount that is difficult to notice, but over a long period of time, the amount of ice lost is quite significant.

   _____

8. The effects of global warming that are beginning to become appar-
    ent include rising sea levels and more powerful storm phenomena.

---

9. It is easy to lose money investing in the stock market because the
    prices of shares on the market can vary widely from one moment
    to the next.

---

10. Many societies engage in massive development projects in order to
    produce objects that are held in high religious regard.

Reading Focus

Inference

MULTIPLE CHOICE

The passage by Jared Diamond is an excerpt from a book. From information in
the excerpt, you can infer points that might be made in the book as a whole.
Circle the choice that best answers each question.

1. Based on the discussion of the Maya at Copan in Paragraph 8,
    which of the following points was most likely made earlier in the
    book?
    a. They intentionally moved soil from hill slopes into valley bot-
        toms to improve farmland.
    b. They cut down forests on hill slopes, which led to soil erosion.
    c. They found ways to prevent soil erosion.
    d. Most of their cities were built on hill slopes.

2. From information in Paragraph 15, which of the following topics
    was most likely discussed earlier in the book as an example of suc-
    cess?
    a. Montana's timber industry
    b. Seattle's colleges
    c. Tikopia's resource management
    d. New Guinea's distant managers

3. Based on the discussion of the Greenland Norse in Paragraph 25, which of the following points was most likely made earlier in the book?

   a. Inuit raids on Norse farms led to the starvation of the Norse.
   b. The Christian Norse society was destroyed in a religious war with the Inuit.
   c. The Inuit lifestyle was better suited to Greenland than the Norse lifestyle.
   d. The Norse in Greenland eventually gave up their Christian religion.

Polysemy

MULTIPLE CHOICE

Each of the words in this exercise is polysemous—it has many meanings. Many of the definitions given for each word are correct. However, only one is the meaning of the word as it is used in the reading. Choose the definition that best explains the word as it is used.

1. *undermine* (Paragraph 6)

   a. weaken the material underneath (something)
   b. weaken (a position of authority) by acting in a way that denies that authority
   c. weaken (as a structure) by digging under in order to cause (the structure's) destruction
   d. weaken (as an argument) by contradicting key supporting points

2. *superficial(ly)* (Paragraph 11)

   a. trivial
   b. external
   c. on the surface
   d. inside

3. *vital* (Paragraph 12)

   a. alive
   b. refreshing
   c. relating to lives
   d. very important

4. *assume* (Paragraph 12)

   a. take (a position)
   b. take as true without certain knowledge
   c. take (control of) forcefully
   d. take on (a false attitude)

5. *offensive* (Paragraph 12)

   a. attacking
   b. causing moral outrage
   c. unpleasant to the senses
   d. stubborn

6. *exhausted* (Paragraph 14)

   a. released in order to empty
   b. used entirely until none are left
   c. very tired
   d. disappeared

7. *comprehended* (Paragraph 19)

   a. included
   b. understood
   c. questioned
   d. discussed

8. *invoking* (Paragraph 26)

   a. calling for help from
   b. calling up through magic
   c. causing
   d. naming as a principle of support for one's actions

Reading Focus
Building a Text Model

IDENTIFYING SUPPORTING DETAILS

This is an outline of a section from the reading (Paragraphs 5–12) about reasons why societies fail to anticipate problems. Without looking at the reading or at your notes, arrange the supporting details into the outline. When you have them in order, look back at the reading and correct any problems. Then, fill in the paragraph numbers for each supporting detail. Note: Supporting details do not necessarily need to be in the order they appear in the reading. If the order is not important to the logical progression of the reading, then you can list them in any order so long as they remain under the correct heading.

a. Americans' embrace of SUVs

b. Chaco Canyon Anasazi's succumbing to drought

c. Classic Lowland Maya's succumbing to drought

d. Deforestation by Maya at Copan

e. Experience forgotten because of a lack of a written record

f. Experience forgotten in spite of a written record

g. French fortifications for World War II

h. Greenland Norse investment in walrus hunting

i. Introduction of rabbits and foxes to Australia

j. Tucson's building of golf courses and watering of gardens

k. Viking misinterpretation of Iceland's soil type

Reasons for failure to anticipate a problem

1. Failure due to lack of experience
    a. _____ Paragraph _____
    b. _____ Paragraph _____
    c. _____ Paragraph _____

2. Failure due to forgotten experience
    a. _____ Paragraph _____
        ii. _____ Paragraph _____
    b. _____ Paragraph _____
        i. _____ Paragraph _____
        ii. _____ Paragraph _____

3. Failure due to reasoning by false analogy
    a. _____ Paragraph _____
    b. _____ Paragraph _____

Putting Reading to Work

WRITING AND DISCUSSION

Read the items and complete the research assignments.

1. The table gives an overview of deforestation in certain countries. Choose one country and do further research about deforestation there. How likely is an environmental collapse—a disaster like those on Easter Island and at Copan? Report your findings in an essay or in an oral presentation.

Worst Deforestation Rate of Primary Forests, 2000–2005. All countries.

Number	Country	Percentage
1	Nigeria	55.7%
2	Viet Nam	54.5%
3	Cambodia	29.4%
4	Sri Lanka	15.2%
5	Malawi	14.9%
6	Indonesia	12.9%
7	North Korea	9.3%
8	Nepal	9.1%
9	Panama	6.7%
10	Guatemala	6.4%

Source: www.mongabay.com, citing data from the United Nations Food and Agriculture Organization. Accessed October 2006.

2. Reasoning by analogy is common in writing that expresses opinions. In an analogy, a writer claims that two things or situations are similar. If the two truly are similar, the analogy is true. If they are not, the analogy is false (see Paragraphs 11–12).

   a. Choose a topic about which opinion writing is common. Some suggestions:
      • the natural environment
      • sources of energy
      • spending money on weapons/wars
      • spending money on schools/education
      • caring for older people

   b. Use an Internet search engine or an in-print index at a library to find articles, letters, blogs, etc., about your topic.

   c. Read several articles (not just one) and look for analogies. List the analogies in the chart.

Situations/Things Being Compared	Analogy True or False?	If False, Why?

3. Do some research in one or two reference sources outside this chapter to gather information about the environmental situation on Easter Island today. You may use print or online sources. Write a one- to two-page report detailing how the situation on Easter Island today is related to the failures mentioned in the reading. As you research, consider these questions.

   • How have the mistakes made by earlier Easter Islanders affected current conditions on the island?
   • Have any of the failures you mentioned in your summary been rectified? If so, how? If not, what has been proposed or what could be done?
   • Have any of these failures led to other problems?

Third Tier: Crime Spree

Pre-Reading

DISCUSSION

In a crime spree, a criminal or group of criminals commit crime after crime. Eventually they are either apprehended in a spectacular climax—or not apprehended at all. This reading deals with a crime spree and with the mistakes the criminal made that led to his arrest. Think about a famous crime spree that you have heard or read about. Before you read, discuss the questions in a small group.

1. What kind of crime did the criminal(s) commit?

2. What sort of personality did the criminal(s) have?

3. What was the motive?

4. Why was the spree successful for so long?

5. How was the criminal or group discovered?

6. How was the criminal or group apprehended?

Reading

The Map Thief[2]

1 The stranger had come to Baltimore's famed Peabody Library on December 7, 1995, with a wish list. It was in a red notebook, roughly the size of a steno pad, its cover bearing the initials U.S.C. and a picture of a gamecock, the mascot for the University of South Carolina, where the man had apparently paid a recent visit. Inside, in neat, well-spaced cursive, was a list of centuries-old books, most of them atlases. Next to many of the titles someone had scribbled the names of various libraries where the books could be found. Several of the entries were followed by "Peabody Inst." or simply "Peabody."

2 Now some of those same books were piled on a desk in the Grand Stack Room. Now the mystery man began to leaf through one of them. Now he stopped to examine a page. Now he took out a razor blade and carefully lowered his hand to the aged paper. . . .

3 Jennifer Bryan, who was then completing her Ph.D. in history at the University of Maryland, had come to the Peabody to work on her dissertation. Her research that day involved scanning volume after volume of British legal documents from the fifteenth and sixteenth centuries. . . . The sound of the library's elevator momentarily drew Bryan's attention, and when the elevator door opened she watched as a librarian took an armful of old volumes to a man sitting across the way. He was the only other patron in the room. . . .

4 She was accustomed to observing other people at libraries. She had been trained to do so. In addition to her graduate work, Bryan was employed as a manuscripts curator at the Maryland Historical Society, located just a few blocks from the Peabody, and part of her job was to keep an eye on the patrons. She knew that there was good reason for such vigilance. Over the past few years rare books rooms all over the country had been plagued by thefts of increasingly valuable antiquities. The Library of Congress, for example, had announced in 1993 that thieves and "slashers" had stolen thousands of items from perhaps five hundred books in its collections. Often those responsible for the thefts did not look like criminals; in a number of cases, in fact, they had been professors, even librarians. And although she had no obvious reason to distrust the man, she began to get an unsettling feeling about him. "Maybe I just have a suspicious nature," she said.

---

[2]From

5 He quickly gave her good reason to worry. "I just happened to look up and over in that direction and thought I saw him tear a page out of a book," she remembered. But it happened so fast, and the man did it with such seeming nonchalance, that at first she did not completely trust her eyes. "I thought, well, *now* what do I do? Do I say something, or did I just imagine that?" . . .

6 By this time, the man had noticed her as well. He kept glancing over his shoulder, flashing her "surreptitious" looks. The man seemed to grow increasingly flustered under her steady stare. "It was weird," she said, "because he must have thought something was up, but he didn't think enough to run, to get out."

7 Instead, he stood up, pulled out a card catalog drawer, and laid it alongside the books, purposefully obstructing Bryan's view. This was a fatal mistake. She could doubt herself no longer. With that one false move, the man had given himself away. . . .

* * *

8 After Jennifer Bryan had told library officials of her concerns about the man, they quietly contacted security officials. Peabody librarian Carolyn Smith then asked the man to move from the Grand Stack Room to a front area, where she hoped to keep an eye on him without arousing his suspicions. The ploy was apparently successful. Even after being moved, the man requested a 1670 atlas of Africa by the cartographer John Ogilby, although perhaps this was simply an attempt to maintain an air of innocence. At any rate, he did not immediately flee—a bad decision. Within a few moments, Donald Pfouts, director of security at the Peabody Institute, had entered the room, joined by two other officers. This time the mystery man decided not to stick around. He grabbed his notebook and walked out the front door, followed by Pfouts and the other security officials.

9 On the library's steps Pfouts said, "Excuse me, sir . . ."

10 The man picked up his pace. The officers walked faster to catch up—and the man hastened his gait to keep ahead of them. In a scene that might have come from some odd amalgamation of *The Nutty Professor* and *The Fugitive*, the bookish desperado now led his pursuers on a slow-speed chase through downtown Baltimore. . . .

11 Searching for an escape route on the far side of the boulevard along Washington Place, the man spotted a 19th century mansion that now serves as a wing of the Walters Art Gallery. Approaching the building he ditched his notebook into a row of shrubbery. Then he climbed a stairway onto the Ionic portico.

12 "The door doesn't go anywhere," Pfouts warned him. The man now realized he was trapped.

13 Pfouts spoke again: "I would really like to invite you back to the library because I think there are some issues here that we have to deal with."

14 When the officers pulled the red spiral notebook from the bushes, they discovered that Jennifer Bryan's suspicions had been well-founded. Folded into its pages were four two-hundred-year-old maps.

* * *

15 Although the staff at the Peabody Library didn't know it at the time, the man they caught with the maps in his notebook also had a compulsion for creating imaginary creatures. The latest—the one whose face appeared on a fake University of Florida student ID card he had presented at the front desk—was named James Perry. But, according to police and court transcripts, there had been many others: James J. Edwards and James Morgan and Jason Pike and Jack Arnett and Richard M. Olinger and John David Rosche and Steven M. Spradling and James Bland.

16 He was no stranger to libraries. In the 1970s, when he was in his twenties, he had visited them often. But this, apparently, was long before he was interested in maps. According to one source who knew him at the time, he would use the libraries to track down the names of people who had died in childhood. Then he would create new identities, using the birth dates of the deceased.

17 He would invent these creatures, and then he would figure out ways to get people to send them free money. It worked for a while but then stopped working so well. In September 1973 the San Diego police arrested a man named Jason Michael Pike for grand theft. The charge, as the man would later admit in court, stemmed from the fact that "I applied for a credit card, and I used it to get money under false pretenses." . . .

18 His real name, pretenses aside, was Gilbert Joseph Bland, Jr. . . . On December 31, 1975, Bland was arrested in Tampa, Florida, for using those identities to defraud the U.S. government in a scheme to collect unemployment compensation for ex-servicemen. He pleaded guilty in U.S. district court, where he was given a three-year sentence and shipped off to the federal corrections institution in El Reno, Oklahoma. He did not like it there, and when he got out he apparently vowed to begin anew.

19 He cut ties with his old family, started a new one, got a college degree, found work in the computer business, and began to lead a middle-class existence in suburban Maryland. . . .

* * *

20 One of the conceits of old mapmakers was to put vigorously huffing classical deities or cherubs in the maps' margins at the cardinal points.

Fair winds or foul? The answer to this question has determined the fate of many a journey—even, perhaps, Gilbert Bland's own odd version of an epic adventure. And up until that day in downtown Baltimore, we can only conclude that the gods had been extremely kind to our mysterious hero. Zephyrus and his brothers had ushered him safely to and fro across the continent, with stops in Seattle and Charlottesville and Chicago and Vancouver and several other apparent ports of plunder. He had been lucky. Any of a million little things could have failed him—a fumbled razor blade, an inopportune rustling of paper, an unseen security camera—but, miraculously, everything had gone off without a hitch. Or maybe he considered it a matter not of miracles but of his own skill. Maybe, as he emerged undetected from the tenth, eleventh, twelfth, thirteenth, fourteenth, or fifteenth library, he began to feel invincible—or, even more intoxicating to him, invisible. Yes, that seems right: he was suffering from hubris, that prideful arrogance which spelled doom for so many a hero of Greek tragedy, causing him to ignore warnings that might have averted disaster.

21 Now it was too late for warnings. The winds had changed, and three foreboding figures suddenly stood before Gilbert Bland on the steps of the Walters Art Gallery. To you and me those three would have looked like slightly exhausted security guards. But Bland could be excused if, in his panic and confusion, they suddenly seemed like creatures surreal and terrifying, with whetted talons ready to tear him asunder. When the Baltimore city police arrived at the Peabody Library a short while later, they found a suspect who was sheepish and scared and apparently ready to cooperate. He admitted his name was not James Perry, as indicated on the University of Florida ID card he had presented to library officials earlier in the day. (Like the name, the card would prove to be a complete fake.) His real identity, he confessed, was Gilbert Joseph Bland, Jr., and he showed police and security officials a Florida driver's license bearing that name. According to library staff members, the man offered no other excuse for taking the maps than that he "just wanted them."

22 It must have seemed to him just then that there was no way out. He had been caught red-handed with stolen maps, sliced from one of the books he was known to have examined earlier in the day, a 1763 work entitled *The General History of the Late War*. A reliable witness had seen the crime take place, and fingerprint and handwriting evidence would almost certainly further tie him to the scene. Then, to his incredulous surprise, the police started talking about letting him go.

23 In his desperation Bland had offered to pay the library—on the spot and in cash—to repair the damaged books, and the cops seemed to think it was a pretty good deal. They had more important things to worry about than Gilbert Bland. Murders had risen nearly 9 percent in the city and its

surrounding counties in the first nine months of 1995, compared with the same period of the previous year. Robbery, aggravated assault, and other crime categories were also on the rise. Nor was the Mount Vernon neighborhood, which had once been among the city's most exclusive enclaves, immune from the problem. Tourists, students, and suburbanites—drawn to the area by attractions such as the famous Peabody Conservatory of Music—were often targeted for robbery or worse.

24 No wonder the officers did not seem particularly concerned about the meek and skittish man they found at the library. Well-dressed, polite, and obviously humiliated, he looked about as much like a menace to society as the Peabody Library looked like a crack house. And after all, what had he allegedly done? Taken a few pages out of a book? Stolen *four sheets of paper*? There were dangerous people out there—crazy, desperate, dangerous people with guns. This poor guy hardly seemed worth the bother. . . .

25 Wouldn't accepting the money in lieu of Bland's immediate arrest be easier for everyone involved? The library would get its book repaired; the crook would learn a frightening and costly lesson; the police would have that much less paperwork, that much more time to focus on real criminals. For their part, library officials thought the idea was at least worth considering. They telephoned a lawyer and mulled over their options, Gilbert Bland's fate still blowing in the wind. . . .

* * *

26 After conferring with security officials, one of the Peabody's top lawyers, Frederick DeKuyper, signed off on a plan to forgo Bland's arrest in return for seven hundred dollars in damages. The suspect, who was reportedly carrying large amounts of cash, was more than happy with the deal. With the gods apparently smiling down upon him once again, he fled the library in a hurry—too much of a hurry, as it turned out. Bland had left his red notebook behind. Within minutes of the thief's departure, the Peabody's security chief, Donald Pfouts, noticed the book and decided to give it a closer examination. He quickly made a discovery that would send shock waves through libraries all over America. . . .

27 Now let us consider a work by the famous sculptor and architect Robert Mills, who designed the District of Columbia's Washington Monument, for one. . . . He also drew the maps for the 1825 *Atlas of the State of South Carolina*. It was not only a beautiful piece of art in its own right but a work of real historical importance—the first state atlas ever produced in the United States. . . . Although the public at large knows virtually nothing—and cares even less—about the *Atlas of the State of South Carolina*, a small number of map collectors and dealers value it a great deal. Today a

copy of the atlas in excellent condition might sell for upwards of $30,000. A single map of Charleston County from the atlas might fetch $2,000 or more. And, unfortunately, what collectors and dealers are willing to pay for, thieves are willing to steal.

28 As he flipped through Gilbert Bland's notebook, Donald Pfouts came across the following passage:

For MD Dealer
1. *Currier & Ives (90%)*
2. *Kellogg*
3. *Haskell & Allen*
4. *Baillie*
5. *Mills County Atlas of S.C.*

29 Pfouts could not but recognize the disturbing implications of such words. Almost every page was filled with lists, most of which contained the names of cartographers and the titles of specific maps (and a few of which, such as the preceding example, also included the names of artists and their prints). Next to many of these entries were prices. Pfouts quickly came to a startling conclusion: the notebook was essentially a hit list. Worse yet, there was ample evidence that, far from being an isolated incident, as library officials had assumed, Bland's visit to the Peabody was part of something much bigger. The book contained the names—and, in some cases, addresses—of other libraries where specific maps could be found. Moreover, folded into its pages were informational materials from institutions such as the University of Virginia's Alderman Library, a disturbing clue that other thefts may have already taken place. Then there were those ominous words "For MD Dealer"—a possible implication that the manuscripts were stolen on commission. . . .

30 Peabody librarians went back through their records and discovered that more maps were missing from other texts that Bland had allegedly handled, during both this visit and one the previous September. Four plates were missing from the now decidedly incomplete *Complete Atlas or Distinct View of the Known World* by eighteenth-century cartographer Emanuel Bowen, along with material from works by Mathew Carey, Jacques Nicolas Bellin, Entick, and Pierre-Francois-Xavier de Charlevoix. In all, twenty-seven plates were missing from the Peabody alone. Had other institutions suffered similar losses? It was now becoming frighteningly clear to Hopkins officials that they might be dealing with a crime spree.

31 Cynthia Requardt is special collections curator at the Milton S. Eisenhower Library at Johns Hopkins University in Baltimore. Since 1982, the Peabody Library has been one of those special collections. Requardt had not been in on the decision to free Bland, but she was familiar with all

the details. She began calling the libraries that appeared to have been targeted in the notebook. Then she went to her computer and sent out a message over ExLibris, an electronic discussion group for those interested in rare books and special collections:

> On December 7, Gilbert Joseph Bland, Jr., was apprehended removing maps from eighteenth century books at the George Peabody Library of The Johns Hopkins University in Baltimore.
>
> Bland was using the alias James Perry. He is a white male, 46 years of age, 5'9" or 10", with light brown hair (receding) and a light brown mustache. A photograph is available.
>
> When apprehended, Bland presented a Florida driver's license. In lieu of pressing charges, the library accepted payment for damages, and Bland was released. Since his release, we have reason to believe that Bland has visited other research libraries in the mid-Atlantic region.

32 For Requardt, Pfouts, and other Hopkins officials, there was little to do but wait—and hope that their worst fears would not be realized. . . .

* * *

33 In his own curious quest, Gilbert Bland seems to have had in common with the old breed a certain compulsion toward risk. But for the most part he was solidly of the new breed. In the early 1990s, before turning his interest to maps, Bland ran a computer consulting firm, and he apparently put his technical knowledge to good use during his crime spree. He did not make his actual conquests on the Web, of course. But, according to law enforcement officials, he did do his exploration and discovery there—using the Internet, for example, to track down Ogilby's *America* at the University of Washington. Gary Menges found some bitter irony in that. "You tell the world you have something in order that people are aware of its existence and can come and use it," he said. "And then you have people who are not using this information for scholarly purposes. They're using it to put together their hit lists."

34 But if the death of distance helped Bland to stalk libraries, it also helped the libraries hunt down Bland. In the past, word of his apprehension in Baltimore would have traveled slowly, through gossip and other largely informal channels. But thanks to Cynthia Requardt's posting on ExLibris—a news group established in 1990 for discussion of rare books and manuscripts librarianship—institutions all over the country received notice of the crime only hours after it had taken place. . . .

35 Added John E. Ingram of the University of Florida, "What I find to be the most difficult part is to realize that someone was coming in and destroying part of our heritage. We are a state institution, and the person who took the maps was robbing the entire state and the country, not just the library. For instance, for one of the titles—*Modern History, or, the Present State of All Nations* by Thomas Salmon—we have the only complete copy in the state of Florida. Well, we formerly had the only complete copy." . . .

36 Capturing Bland again did not prove to be a simple matter. After being detained in Baltimore, he apparently stayed on for a few days in his old hometown of Columbia, Maryland. While there, he called the Peabody Institute's security chief, Donald Pfouts, to request the return of his notebook. "He said he forgot his book and he really needed to get it," explained Pfouts. "Once he found out he wasn't getting his book back, I think that's when he really realized what the possibilities were. And that's when he fled."

37 It would take law enforcement officials nearly a month to capture him. . . . Bureaucracy, indifference, and disorganization can be more difficult to navigate than the widest ocean. Although Bland had managed thus far to escape arrest, he had not escaped attention. A number of major media outlets, including the *Baltimore Sun* and Associated Press, had already run stories about the crime spree; many more, including *The Washington Post*, the *Chicago Tribune*, and National Public Radio, would soon follow. . . .

* * *

38 While news of Bland's crime was breaking all over the country, the FBI's attempts to get a search warrant for Bland's map store in Florida had gotten bogged down in red tape. "A search warrant has to be originated in the same jurisdiction that it's going to be executed," explained Special Agent Henry F. Hanburger of the FBI office in Columbia, Maryland. "And timing was terrible with the Christmas holidays and the absence of people at work both on the prosecutor's side and our side. . . . We just couldn't get the needed prosecutor to say, 'Damn right, let's get a search warrant.'"

39 The man who brought Gilbert Bland to justice was neither a high-profile FBI agent nor a flashy detective on a big-city police force. He was a campus cop, not too far up on the law-enforcement food chain from the lowly private security guard. Nonetheless, Thomas W. Durrer had a keen mind and, more important, a roiling sense of curiosity. As an investigator for the University of Virginia (UVA) police department, Durrer was involved mostly in mundane matters such as dormitory break-ins or stolen backpacks. But he took pleasure in the detail work that others might find boring, tracking down all the scattered little pieces of evidence, then putting seemingly unrelated facts together until they told a complete story.

40 In early December 1995, he landed a case that required just such skills. The Alderman Library at UVA reported that at least seven rare maps were missing, including eighteenth-century works by the cartographers Herman Moll and Andrew Ellicott. Librarians had discovered the loss after hearing from Johns Hopkins officials, who had noted references to the Alderman in the map thief's notebook. A check of the records confirmed that someone using the name James Perry had indeed paid visits to the Alderman on December 5 and 6, right before Gilbert Bland's ill-fated stop in Baltimore.

41 By checking with motels near UVA, Durrer eventually found out which credit card "James Perry" was using. Through card records, he managed to trace visits by Bland to numerous university towns throughout the United States, thereby ratcheting up the pressure on the FBI to break the procedural logjam. Durrer didn't actually catch Bland, but he did make his capture happen. A day or two *after* Bland had cleaned out his map store in Tamarac, Florida—stashing its contents who-knew-where—FBI agents tracked him down. And it was not until two weeks later, January 2, 1996, that the map thief turned himself in to local police in Florida. At long last Bland was in custody. Now it was his maps that were nowhere to be found.

Post-Reading

Basic Comprehension

SHORT ANSWER

Use information from the reading to answer the questions in your own words.

1. What was Bland's alleged motive for stealing the maps when he was first discovered? What was his real motive?

   _____

   _____

   _____

2. What did Bland do that contributed to his success?

   _____

   _____

   _____

3. What factors delayed Bland's apprehension?

   _____

   _____

   _____

MULTIPLE CHOICE

Circle the choice that best answers each question.

1. Which statement best expresses the ultimate outcome of Bland's crime spree?

   a. After the Peabody Library, Bland was never seen again and maps continued to disappear.

   b. Bland returned most of what he stole, so he was never punished for his crimes.

   c. Bland was arrested, but most of the works he stole were not recovered.

   d. Police were ultimately able to track down most of the stolen maps at great expense.

2. All of the following are reasons why Jennifer Bryan was particularly likely to notice Bland EXCEPT _____.

   a. many library thefts had occurred recently

   b. she had been trained to watch people working with old manuscripts

   c. she happened to be sitting near him

   d. she worked for the Peabody Library

3. Which of the following most likely explains why the author included the statement that "in a number of cases, in fact, they had been professors, even librarians" (Paragraph 4)?

   a. To decry a recent decline in the morals of academics

   b. To help explain why the criminals did not look suspicious

   c. To give examples of people who are ill-suited to capturing criminals

   d. To provide background on Bland's former occupation

4. What did Bland's pursuers *first* notice when they found his red notebook?

   a. a hit list of atlases

   b. a list of libraries

   c. a record of Bland's former identities

   d. four stolen maps

5. The reading mentions that the hit list in Bland's red notebook
   _____.

   a. contained the names of the people Bland had sold the maps to
   b. was written in the Peabody Library
   c. went unnoticed until after Bland had been allowed to go free from the Peabody Library
   d. was written in a secret code that detectives could not decipher

6. How did Bland use libraries in the early 1970s?

   a. To look for information that would help him create false identities
   b. To research atlases as a professor
   c. To steal old maps and sell them
   d. To study computer science and prepare for his degree

7. What was NOT mentioned as a factor contributing to Bland's release after the Peabody incident?

   a. Bland offered to pay for the damage.
   b. Bland looked harmless.
   c. Police were more concerned with violent crimes.
   d. The Peabody could not get in touch with its lawyers.

8. Why were the words *For MD Dealer* labeled "ominous" by the author?

   a. The words confused officers as to what Bland's real motives were.
   b. The words had been written in larger print than the other words in the notebook.
   c. The words showed that someone other than Bland had put together the list.
   d. The words suggested that someone was intentionally paying Bland to commit the thefts.

9. What phrase best characterizes Bland's thefts on the day he was caught at the Peabody?

   a. the latest in a series of thefts from many libraries
   b. the events that led to a new career for Jennifer Bryan
   c. the events that launched a long criminal career for Bland
   d. the crime that led to big changes in the Baltimore police department

10. Which TWO facts are mentioned in the reading as ways Bland's fate was affected by the Internet?

   a. Bland sold his maps via an online store.
   b. A posting on the Internet alerted librarians to his crimes.
   c. The Internet helped Bland locate his targets.
   d. Police used the Internet to confirm Bland's earlier aliases.

Vocabulary

MULTIPLE CHOICE

Choose the word or phrase closest in meaning to the italicized word(s) in each sentence from the reading.

1. "It was in a red notebook, roughly the size of a steno pad, its cover *bearing* the initials U.S.C. and a picture of a gamecock, the mascot for the University of South Carolina, where the man had apparently paid a recent visit."

   a. having
   b. hiding
   c. holding
   d. covering

2. "Over the past few years rare books rooms all over the country had *been plagued by* thefts of increasingly valuable antiquities."

   a. avoided
   b. discovered
   c. gotten used to
   d. suffered from

3. "The man seemed to grow increasingly *flustered* under her steady stare."

   a. depressed
   b. set on his goal
   c. sure of himself
   d. unsettled

4. "Instead, he stood up, pulled out a card catalog drawer, and laid it alongside the books, purposefully *obstructing* Bryan's view."

   a. blocking
   b. improving
   c. narrowing
   d. permitting

5. "Peabody librarian Carolyn Smith then asked the man to move from the Grand Stack Room to a front area, where she hoped to keep an eye on him without *arousing* his suspicions."

   a. changing
   b. increasing
   c. raising
   d. naming

6. "In a scene that might have come from some odd *amalgamation* of The Nutty Professor and The Fugitive, the bookish desperado now led his pursuers on a slow-speed chase through downtown Baltimore."

   a. imagination
   b. mixture
   c. production
   d. script

7. "Although the staff at the Peabody library didn't know it at the time, the man they caught with the maps in his notebook also had a *compulsion* for creating imaginary creatures."

   a. habit
   b. hobby
   c. strong urge
   d. talent

8. "Yes, that seems right: he was suffering from hubris, that prideful arrogance which spelled doom for so many a hero of Greek tragedy, causing him to ignore warnings that might have *averted* disaster."

   a. predicted
   b. prevented
   c. reduced
   d. reversed

9. "Wouldn't accepting the money *in lieu of* Bland's immediate arrest be easier for everyone involved?"

   a. as a result of
   b. for
   c. in addition to
   d. instead of

10. "On December 7, Gilbert Joseph Bland, Jr., was *apprehended* removing maps from eighteenth century books at the George Peabody Library of The Johns Hopkins University in Baltimore."

    a. caught
    b. recorded
    c. seen
    d. suspected of

11. "Almost every page was filled with lists, most of which contained the names of *cartographers* and the titles of specific maps (and a few of which, such as the preceding example, also included the names of artists and their prints)."

    a. artists
    b. bookmakers
    c. libraries
    d. mapmakers

MATCHING

Match each italicized word or phrase on the left with the phrase on the right that most closely relates to it. <u>Note</u>: Two of the italicized words mean the same thing.

1. a situation in which one might exhibit *nonchalance* _____

2. an *ill-fated* trip _____

3. an *ominous* event _____

4. a *foreboding* sight _____

5. a *mundane* activity _____

6. a *high-profile* figure _____

7. something that might make one feel *humiliated* _____

8. a *meek* figure _____

9. something *skittish* _____

10. an *exclusive* organization _____

a. a club that will only accept new members that all are approved by current members

b. a horse in the presence of a rattlesnake

c. a wolf with teeth bared and hair raised

d. brushing one's teeth in the morning

e. making a huge mistake

f. someone who speaks softly and doesn't make eye contact

g. a hurricane

h. the maiden voyage of the *Titanic*

i. the president of a country

j. when one is trying to cover up a lie

FIGURATIVE LANGUAGE

Figurative phrases make colorful, interesting images. They often have meanings that are different from what their words actually say. Match the italicized figurative phrases and sentences with their literal meanings in the list on page 231. If the phrases contain cultural references with which you are unfamiliar, do some research to figure them out.

1. "*Zephyrus and his brothers had ushered him* safely *to and fro* across the continent" _____

2. "several other apparent *ports of plunder*" _____

3. "*The winds had changed*" _____

4. "they suddenly seemed like *creatures surreal and terrifying, with whetted talons ready to tear him asunder*" _____

5. "He had been caught *red-handed* with stolen maps" _____

6. "*He looked about as much like a menace to society as the Peabody Library looked like a crack house*" _____

7. "*With the gods apparently smiling down* upon him once again" _____

8. "Gilbert Bland seems to have had in common with *the old breed* a certain compulsion toward risk" _____

9. "But if *the death of distance* helped Bland to stalk libraries, it also helped the libraries hunt down Bland." _____

10. "But if the death of distance helped Bland to *stalk* libraries, it also helped the libraries hunt down Bland." _____

11. "But if the death of distance helped Bland to stalk libraries, it also helped the libraries *hunt down* Bland." _____

12. "The FBI's attempts to get a search warrant for Bland's map store in Florida had gotten *bogged down in red tape*." _____

13. "*not too far up on the* law-enforcement *food chain from* the lowly private security guard" _____

14. "*ratcheting up* the pressure on the FBI to break the procedural logjam" _____

15. "ratcheting up the pressure on the FBI to *break the* procedural *logjam*" _____

a. appeared very non-threatening

b. circumstances were different

c. delayed by bureaucratic procedures

d. ease of finding information on the Internet

e. extremely threatening figures

f. find for the purpose of apprehension

g. had moved around with good fortune

h. increasing step-by-step

i. keep track of for malicious purposes

j. old-fashioned criminals

k. places from which he stole

l. remove that which is preventing action

m. with clear evidence of guilt

n. with good luck

o. with little authority

Reading Focus

Textual Organization

Overall, the reading is a narrative (a story) that begins on December 7, 1995, and ends on January 2, 1996. Most of the reading is a straight narrative; it presents events chronologically, from earliest to latest, within that period. However, some parts of the reading are flashbacks, in which the story jumps back to some earlier time.

Typically, a paragraph has one main purpose—either to carry the narrative forward or to flash back. Even if the paragraph contains both straight narrative and flashbacks, one or the other is more important. For example, consider Paragraph 1. It starts the straight narrative and also mentions actions from the past (visiting the University of South Carolina; writing in the notebook). Its main purpose, however, is clearly to carry forward the straight narrative. The earlier actions are mentioned only to help describe the situation on December 7, 1995.

STRAIGHT NARRATIVE AND FLASHBACKS

In the table, the paragraphs of the reading are divided into seven sections according to topic divisions in the reading. Complete the chart to show whether each paragraph is meant to be mostly straight narrative (SN) or flashback (FB). Identify the time(s) referred to in any flashback(s). The first one is done for you as an example. Then discuss your answers with one or more other students.

Paragraph	SN/FB	Time(s) of Flashback(s)
SECTION 1		
1	SN	
2	SN	
3	SN	
4	FB	Jennifer Bryan's training; when libraries were robbed
SECTION 2		
8		
9		
10		
11		
12		
13		
SECTION 3		
14		
15		
16		
17		
SECTION 4		
18		
19		
20		
21		
22		
23		
24		

SECTION 5		
25		
26		
27		
28		
29		
30		
SECTION 6		
31		
32		
33		
SECTION 7		
34		
35		
36		
37		
38		
39		

ORDER OF EVENTS

Write numbers from 1 to 12 to show the chronological order of these events from the reading. Mark 1 for the earliest and 12 for the latest.

a. _____ Jennifer Bryan sees Bland tear a page out of a book.

b. _____ A librarian moves Bland to a different room in the library.

c. _____ A librarian posts a notice about Bland's activities via an Internet discussion group.

d. _____ Robert Mills draws maps for an atlas.

e. _____ Bland goes to prison for defrauding the U.S. government.

f. _____ Dan Pfouts realizes that Bland's theft from the Peabody was part of a series of thefts.

g. _____ Security officers catch Bland on a stairway to an art gallery.

h. _____ Bland gets a college degree.

i. _____ The Peabody allows Bland to go free after paying for the damage he caused.

j. _____ "James Perry" visits the library at the University of Virginia.

k. _____ Bland tries using a catalog card drawer to hide his actions.

l. _____ Bland turns himself in to police in Florida.